PHARMACIES
CONSTRUCTION AND DESIGN MANUAL

PHARMACIES
CONSTRUCTION AND DESIGN MANUAL

Editor: Dörte Becker †, Philipp Meuser
Scientific advisor: Prof. Franz Labryga
Coauthors: Prof. Dr. Klaus Bergdolt, Klaus R. Bürger

DOM
publishers

INDEX

The colours flow fluidly from a soft blue into orange, and then into red and green. As many glances as the shop window attracts during the day, in the dark it is an absolute eyecatcher, even at a distance. One could almost believe that it is a light installation produced by art students trying to draw attention to grievances at their university.

Not all that long ago, the local pharmacy was still solidly fitted out with wooden furniture. The pharmacy still had the appearance of a workshop for health, where, in keeping with centuries-old tradition, the pharmacist was a craftsman who continued to produce some medicines himself. This practical experience in handling the materia medica produced an in-house manufactured insecticide, which was excellent in every respect. So everything was as it should be: The pharmacy employees were competent and friendly; the atmosphere was simple and pleasant – just like being in the corner shop; trust in the pharmacist's expertise existed on the basis of precisely such alchemical brews as the insecticide. For me, at least, the "apothecary's shop" had proved itself to be more than just a storehouse (Greek: apo = away and tithenai = lay) for a range of goods and a hatch for passing through prescribed drugs. Suddenly, however, the old, familiar pharmacy was closed down. Subsequently this new pharmacy, designed in white and enhanced by warm light colours, was opened, as if out of thin air. There

was no longer a clear physical separation between the pharmacist, as an expert adviser, and the customer on the other side – only a mental division. After all, the pharmacist knows that his position of privilege has been accorded to him step by step under law since the 12th/13th century, and that his practical, craftsmanlike profession has been recognised as an academic discipline since the 19th century. According to representative surveys undertaken by various opinion research institutes, alongside doctors, pharmacists enjoy an undiminished level of trust amongst the German public, with a rate of 84 to 93 percent. "Ask your doctor or pharmacist" is not only a slogan to warn against the side effects of certain medicines, but is also a formula aimed at arousing trust based on specialist expertise. The ladies and gentlemen in white coats as an outpost of the medical practice, who serve as its extended arm, are well aware of the respectful distance which the patients as customers accord them by virtue of their office. This means that the line separating the customer from the pharmacy's specialist, private area, once represented by the sales counter, can now be relaxed in optical and constructional terms. Only the window at the night service counter remains as it was.

Under law, pharmacies are obliged to ensure that in the public interest, the population is adequately supplied with medicines. In order to practice their profession, pharmacists are required to obtain a licence. The ever-present trust in the art

PHILIPP MEUSER

THE HEALTH DESIGNERS
PHARMACIES CAUGHT BETWEEN PROFESSIONAL TRADITION AND THE MODERN MARKET

of the pharmacist has been legally guaranteed under law since the 13th century by controls imposed by the authorities. In this way, the pharmacist was protected from the competition of hawkers, miracle healers, and other charlatans. Has any pharmacist ever gone bust under the described system?

One of the last guild privileges to be preserved in today's modern market and consumer society also entails monitoring. Names such as "Ratsapotheke", "Hofapotheke", "Klosterapotheke", and "Spitalapotheke" (city, court, monastery, and hospital apothecary) demonstrate the prestige of pharmacies for the cities and territorial authorities, be they spiritual or secular. Frequently, outstanding architects were commissioned with the construction and interior decoration of these pharmacies. That many of them possessed luxurious furnishings was simply a matter of good taste. It is therefore nothing new that pharmacies were lent an identity, or a confirmed reputation, through location, furnishings, or quality of craftsmanship. The court doctor and apothecary formed an essential double act which was responsible for the well-being and health of His Grace and his family - precisely because of the already proven professional expertise. One could not train to become a court or city apothecary, one achieved this status by appointment. The pharmacy as a location therefore only reflected the respect which the pharmacist's skills had earned.

The pharmacy as designer shop

The difference to today lies in the egalitarianism of pharmacies. The aristocracy has fallen, the royal households have been abolished, and city councils no longer have their own pharmacist with corresponding premises. Pharmacists and their business premises are part of a great whole beneath the pharmacy sign reserved for guild members, and as such they are already privileged. How, therefore, can an individual member of a free profession amidst a network of 21,500 pharmacists make himself stand out and - above all - in comparison with whom? As made clear by the *Federal Union of German Associations of Pharmacists*, competition and danger threaten not from amongst their own ranks, but rather from outside - and in several respects, as well.

In a sophisticated culture such as ours where, in the public perception, medicine has practically banished illness - thus also its worst case scenario: death - and it is now a question of remaining healthy, that means young and full of vitality, for as long as possible, the pharmacist's role has changed. Nobody goes to the pharmacy anymore because of questions of life and death - or at least if they do, they don't let it show. What people go to the pharmacy for is to register for a yoga course, or holistic healing, or to buy a dietary supplement. The trend which is changing and will continue to change pharmacies is known as "wellness". This is the word,

written in large, clear letters that one sees first in the window of the local pharmacy on the corner. And it is this sense of well-being that determines the fit-out. The trend is towards a health system which spends a fortune on the luxuries of "forever young" and "living forever" and has allowed these to penetrate the system at every level. Even the statutory health insurance funds have erased illness from their self-image, and have exchanged it for the fresh scent of flowers and the happy faces of naturally healthy people. It's a question of health. "Health fund" or "the enterprise of life" are the new advertising slogans. So the change lies in the system.

The other change is the market which results out of this. Thanks to the trend described above, the pharmacies' product ranges are competing on this level with health food stores and drugstores. This is the result and is down to the fact that the classical pharmacies are suddenly competing with health food stores and drugstores, as well as completely new types of pharmacy such as branch outlets of certain companies like *DocMorris*, the international pharmaceutical mail-order company, or online sales with their incredible aggressive pricing policies.

However, it is the citizen himself who decides. Green awareness has not only given many people to understand - at least theoretically - that man is part of a greater natural diversity, but has also led to a new physical awareness. In contrast to orthodox medicine, the so-called alternative

1-3 Leibniz-Apotheke, Berlin
Illuminated display window of
a pharmacy.

healing methods and practices which treat physical ailments based on the idea of the person as a body-mind-spirit being have discredited the pharmacist as a public supplier of pharmaceuticals, which are prescribed by doctors and produced in the laboratories of chemical companies.

The orthodox medical troika of doctor, pharmaceutical industry, and pharmacist as the pharma vendor no longer functions. The cause lies with the citizen whose awareness has been heightened, thus offering him a choice with regard to the concept he wants to use to become or remain healthy. Surveys notwithstanding, the orthodox school of medicine is tarnished and the pharmacist who is right in the middle has a problem. The visible and undeniable strength of nature, its healing plants, and the substances extracted from them are just as much in demand as is knowledge about the body's powers of self-healing. In the midst of all this, the pharmacist's expertise as an advisor and person of trust, traditionally developed through practical experience and sanctified with academic titles, is asserting itself more than ever before. There is also the cash crisis within the health system. Medicines from the pharmaceutical companies are becoming more expensive and the health funds are nearing financial collapse. The orthodox exploitation chain of pharmaceutical industry, doctor, pharmacist, and customer is also financially creaky, compared with the affordable competition from mail-order and online purchasing which is aggressive and highly successful. This is why the pharmacy has diversified from being a legally privileged dispensary of prescription medicines, into a store for natural healing remedies and health consultancy. The binding force between all of these elements is expertise, that means training and certification.

Architecture as a creator of identity
In a market where, on the one hand, borders are blurring and, on the other, its privileges are being removed, just like any other business pharmacies need to demonstrate quality to the outside world and make their own role – apart from certified privileges – visible. The magic formula is "corporate identity", which must be visible both from a distance and on entering the pharmacy with regard to attitude, behaviour, and the communication of specialist skills, all the way through to the internal organisation. It is a question of corporate design. "Who am I, where am I, what am I, what do I have to offer?" All of these questions concerning the pharmacy should be answered clearly for all the senses by architecture. For these are precisely the questions to which the customer expects an answer, which he subconsciously registers and which help him to decide whether to go into the pharmacy or not. The range of designed identity extends from the business's own logo and all communication material, to the design of the business and the corresponding internet platform.

The architect has to bear all of these elements in mind because, as with any other provider of branded goods, this is an issue which involves nothing less than creating instant brand recognition, a question of ensuring and intensifying the customer's identification with "his pharmacy". It is the coherent unity of all these elements which allow a pharmacy to create a good external impression.

Inside, the colours, materials, and structure need to be coordinated. A restrainedly elegant and harmonious use of all three elements is essential here. Designing a pharmacy is, first and foremost, the job of the interior designer. It is evident that it is the offices who are equally at home with the disciplines of design, interior design, and architecture, who predominantly prove best at designing pharmacies. Or the designers may also be architects who have adequately demonstrated skills of the highest order in other areas such as living, gastronomy, offices, commercial premises or in defferent selected sectors.

The underlying design rule is: "Form follows content and function". In other words, a clear shape vocabulary and superior materials are required, and the two must be combined to create an atmosphere of integrity, as well as a spatial separation between the customer area and the pharmacy's working areas. A pharmacy is not a drugstore, and its design is required to meet the demands of a designer store – for example

an optician's shop. This is because, in keeping with their professional claim to provide expert guidance and specialist knowledge as the customer's person of trust, the pharmacy ranks in the premium league of retail trade. Based on their products, pharmacies are superior sales outlets. They have to be – and that's the way their furnishings have to look as well. Design details are oriented to the size, location, and contentual self-image of the pharmacy.

Apart from having friendly personnel who are highly skilled at what they do, a good pharmacy primarily distinguishes itself externally through the use of colour. At a time when even delivery rooms and hospitals or medical practices are decorated in cheerful colours, nobody wants to go into a pharmacy that is chalk-white. As far back as 1791 Johann Wolfgang von Goethe was already examining the effect of colours on people's behaviour and mood. We have the Brazilian theologian Dom Hélder Pessoa Câmara to thank for the following finding, formulated in simple yet moving words: "The light which falls on things transforms them." Therefore, for a professionally designed pharmacy, the choice of colour for floor, ceiling, walls, and furnishings is elemental for the design of the spatial atmosphere, whereby the effect of external light and the reproduction of colours by means of artificial light should also be considered. It is a question of atmosphere. If this is right, and goes hand in hand with competent advice that creates trust, and friendly, skilled service, the pharmacy has won: both the customer and the turnover. If the first is not right, all the expertise in the world is of little or no use. Dark shades for the floor ensure that the customer feels looked after and secure. A change from dark to light flooring makes it possible to show the border between the public area and that of the personnel. The colours used should be calming and solid, and this should extend to the furniture, as a relaxing atmosphere is also an aid to well-being. If restrained background and material colours are also used, what is truly central will automatically become the focus of attention: the products.

It is important that these materials are correctly chosen. Because the pharmacist as a profession has a longstanding tradition, materials should be chosen which will age gracefully. Nothing is worse than a dispensary which looks like a DIY store. A corporate culture is a thing of lasting value which, like wine or love, matures with age, and should never be allowed to become tarnished. Fashion trends come and go, but a good pharmacy is like a mature individual, who is serene in himself, regardless of trends. Change may, at most, emerge out of the pharmacy's own corporate self-image.

4-10 Leibniz-Apotheke, Berlin
Illuminated display window of
a pharmacy.

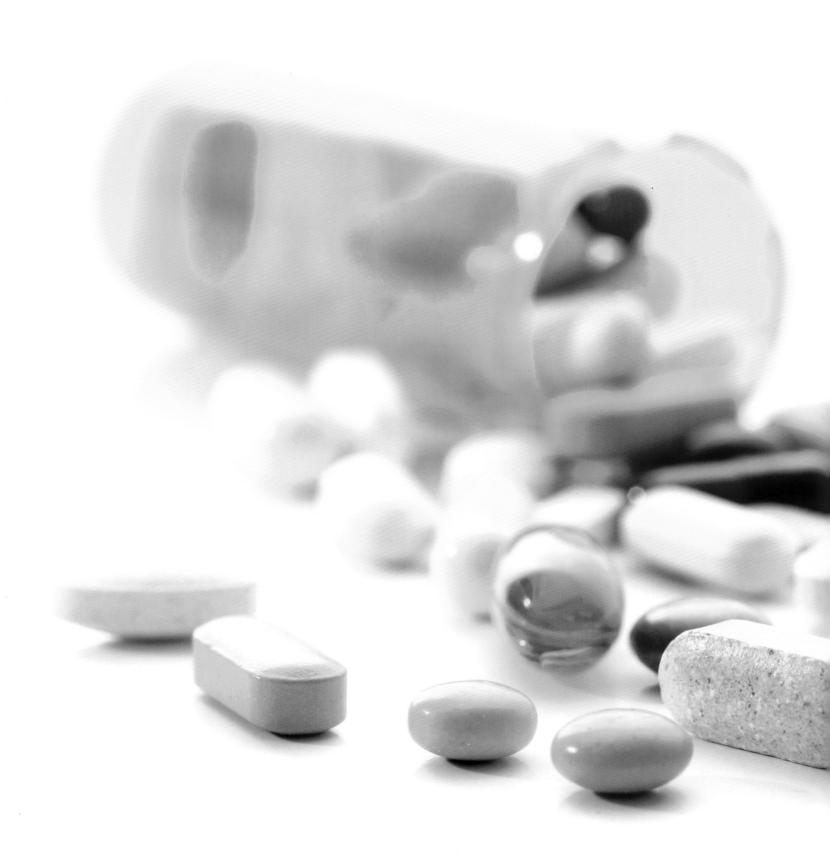

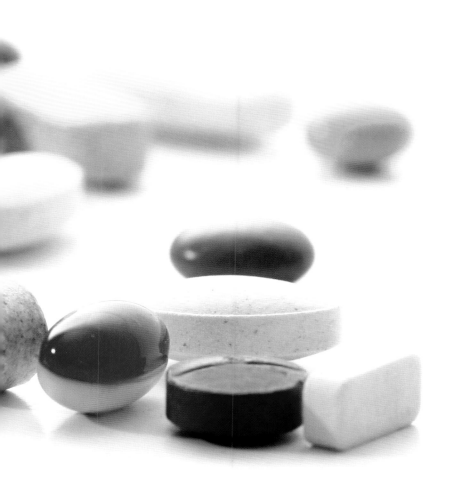

Old pharmacies exercise a huge fascination over many people. In many places they have been lovingly refurbished and their original appearance restored, so that one can sense how people in the Middle Ages and the early Modern era must have felt when entering such places. Hidden away behind artistically numbered drawers, beneath tables, in boxes, tins, mortars, retorts, leather pouches, distilling apparatus and bottles, in secret cupboards or poison cabinets were those substances with which the apothecary [as the pharmacist was once known] mixed his medicines. It was not merely a question of assisting the individual in his everyday, often fruitless attempt to cure serious illnesses – the apothecary also sought cures for plagues which threatened both man and beast, for diseases which brought war in their wake, and for risks to the life and limb of the rulers.

For centuries, the apothecary's shop was a "workshop for health", mysterious and with a magical aura. In the view of the simple people, alchemy and magic were tangibly close there; and where else would one expect the manufacture of gold, or the creation of the "homunculus" than somewhere like a apothecary's shop whose technical equipment was more or less predestined for such uses? Following doctor's prescriptions or based on the apothecary's own imagination and expertise, pills, creams, drops, infusions, emetics, comfits, suppositories, embrocations, cosmetics, and herbal mixtures for both internal and external use were expertly prepared. The apothecary's expert knowledge was equal to the doctor's when it came to medication ["materia medica"]; there is documentary evidence that rivalry already existed between the two disciplines in the Middle Ages. The gathering, drying, crushing, distilling, and colouring of medical plants and substances said to have curative properties, provided first practical experience. What they tended to lack was the theory, that means physicians trained with regard to plants and healing herbs using the works of antique and medieval authors. Until into the 19th century, there was no standard training for pharmacists, so that their number included respected natural scientists, as well as harmless hucksters and respectable artisans.

In general, however, access to the apothecary's shop appeared almost hermetic, something that was further reinforced by Latin inscriptions and enigmatic shorthand. That they were often housed beneath ancient vaults or in cellars strengthened this impression still further. The alchemical tradition, that of searching for the "quintessence" of things, the barely disputed existence of miracle pills, the collecting of gemstones, unicorn horn powder, bezoar stone, or the mysterious, human-shaped mandragora – all of these aroused astonishment and, indeed, fear. "Dosis facit venenum" – danger is simultaneously implicit in the old principle of healing: What was useful

KLAUS BERGDOLT

FROM HERB GARDEN TO MAIL-ORDER PHARMACY
HISTORIC FACTS ABOUT THE PHARMACY

or did good, what could preserve life could also – if wrongly administered – lead to death. Poisons and their antidotes have frighteningly common properties, and every visitor sensed this. That "Composita" had strength greater than the sum of their parts, and that "Simplicia" possessed an additional "Vis occulta" had already been stressed by Galen and Avicenna. Life and death, salvation and danger rubbed shoulders on the shelves, so that weighing scales and measuring unit took on a special significance. A beautiful apothecary's shop demonstrated nothing less than the cultural standing of the given municipality. Indeed, without the dispensing of medicines, doctors' efforts to preserve health were condemned to failure. Apothecaries, irrespective of the diversity of their training, enjoyed a very special level of trust amongst the people; an important quality which also reaped great rewards. Since time immemorial, apothecaries have been crucial advisors, as were those drug and root traders who took on the role of apothecary where none was available.

In early Modern times, from 1600 to 1800, the various types of apothecary [city council apothecary, court apothecary, monastery apothecary, or infirmary apothecary] were objects of prestige belonging to the municipalities, princes or clerics. Not infrequently, outstanding architects were commissioned with their design and construction. Many possessed noble, almost luxurious furnishings, which fulfilled all possible aesthetic demands. Magnificent examples have been preserved, predominantly from the 18th century – from Portugal to Russia. The court apothecary in particular enjoyed high status for centuries and, just like the personal physician, accompanied the prince or king with his "travelling apothecary", a beautifully crafted portable cabinet, which contained space for small bottles, cinnamon canisters, tins of unguent, and even books. The idea of the apothecary's shop as the central place for the production and sale of medication, separate from a medical practice, had already been born in the high Middle Ages. It is likely that the example was set by the Arabs, although such establishments also existed in Byzantium. Pharmacological literature which not only legitimised the profession of apothecary, but also elevated its authority, can be traced back to ancient times. Works ascribed to Theophrastus, Pliny, Galen, and Dioscurides already had a legendary, almost axiomatic status. No less influential at the time were Avicenna's "Canon Medicinae", the "Antidotarium Nicolai", and a work known as "Circa instans", ascribed to the Italian physician Matthaeus Platearius. It was above all in the monasteries of the early Middle Ages that healing with plants and pharmaceuticals enjoyed great popularity. The floor plan of St. Gallen monastery [around 800] already foresaw a building for physicians and apothecaries ["armarium pigmentorum"]. Almost every monastery had a herb garden, and this is now once again in fashion. An important element here was "signature reading": It was believed that the therapeutic effectiveness of a plant could be recognised from its external shape and colour.

It was above all in the 13th century that early forms of the pharmacy, that means shops for medicines, were established in many European cities. The expanding international trade in drugs and herbs [Byzantium, Venice, Pisa, Nuremberg] had a crucial influence on this development. Whether the professional pharmacist ultimately developed out of the monasteries or from the guild of travelling drug traders ["huckster theory"] is still debated today. It were precisely the exotic, imported healing substances, whose origins possessed an aura of the legendary, which were considered to be highly effective, at latest since the Carolingian period. From the 14th century, apothecaries were sworn in by urban or state authorities; firstly in Italy and southern Europe and then later, north of the Alps, state concessions for establishing apothecaries were granted. The "Assizes" of the Norman king, Roger II [1140], ratified at the assembly of Ariano, contained the first [preserved] European Apothecary's Code. This was followed – firstly for the Italian-ruled area – by Frederick II of Hohenstaufen's "Constitutiones medicales" [1231]. In the West, pharmacy was now considered to be an independent science, separate from medicine, but equally necessary. This did not prevent

Important substances are extracted from healing plants.
1 Sage (Salvia officinalis)
2 Peppermint (Mentha x piperita)
3 Stinging nettle (Urtica dioica)

that, in fact, it was practised more as a skilled trade. Regular inspections of apothecaries, as were prescribed in the Venetian "Capitulare de specialibus" [1258], were soon obligatory, but the prices were only partially fixed by the authorities. Apothecaries were generally considered to be free traders. However, stringent restrictions [oath, fixed prices, punishment for violations] were foreseen in the "Breslau Medical Code" of 1352. In central Europe, too, those wishing to open an apothecary's shop generally required a licence. Until the 19th century, most apothecary's shops were astonishingly small, their core elements formed by folding tables, a fireplace, a few cupboards, and a small storeroom.

The term "aphothecarius" is only documented in central Europe since the middle of the 14th century. This was then the master of the apothecary's shop or his deputy. Prior to 1300 there is documentary evidence of apothecaries – in the later, "pharmacist" sense of the word – in only a few German cities for example [1190 in Cologne, 1241 in Trier, 1275 in Mainz]. One special form was the northern German-Hanseatic "city council apothecary" [Ratsapotheke], a "wholesale business" for the sale of drugs and medication of all types, owned by the city itself. In Italy, for example in Florence, apothecaries ["speziali"] were for a long time members of the same guild as doctors and painters – the mixing of herbs, medicines and

colours being seen as a common feature. Since the income of many apothecaries was not very high, they also traded in candles, culinary herbs, cosmetics, amulets, and even relics. There were high penalties for forgeries. In most southern European countries, the training of apothecaries corresponded with the guild rules for skilled tradesmen in the late Middle Ages. Except in the monastery apothecaries, apprentices, journeymen, and masters all worked side by side in Italian apothecaries. Irrespective of this artisanal structure, a certain knowledge of Latin was required. In Germany too, the nature of the profession remained typical. In the late Middle Ages, the master examination was taken in Cologne and was attended by a member of the university's medical faculty. The "materia medica" [term dates back to Dioscurides] prepared in the apothecary comprised a huge range of raw materials which could be processed into medicine. Paracelsus [1493–1541] radically updated the theory of "materia medica". Illnesses were no longer considered to be the result of the wrong mixture of humours, but rather as local changes, which disturbed the organism as a whole, whose chemical processes were controlled by a life force ["Archaeus"]. Illnesses were to be fought with chemical medication, so that tinctures, extracts, essences – produced on the basis of chemical processes – took on a crucial role. Naturally, Paracelsus's theory met with resistance. The Leiden medical professor

Franciscus Sylvius [1614–1672] proposed a compromise which, although it assumed that chemical fermentation processes took place in the body, equated health with the correct balance of acid and alkali, which was influenced by these fermentations. This "clinical chemistry", whose founder is said to be Sylvius, was combined with the old teaching of "euchrasy" and/or the theory of the humours. Pharmacy became ever more complicated—and today it after all remains a chemistry-oriented profession.

In the 16th and 17th centuries, the number of healing plants known in Europe grew rapidly. In the newly founded botanical gardens [such as in Padua, Pisa, Florence and Leiden], exotic growths were planted which had been imported from America and other colonies, and these were then integrated into the established canon of healing plants. However, the professionals often argued about their effects; exotic forgeries were common. Conservative doctors and medical faculties rejected the new plants out of hand. Both doctors and pharmacists long debated whether the traditional mercury cure or rather guajak wood imported from America should be the preferred choice for treating syphilis, a disease which was brought by Charles VIII's army from France to central Europe [hence "the French disease"].

Around 1500, the invention of printing encouraged the production of detailed herbal books, which popularised botanical and pharmaceutical knowledge to a certain extent. The

works of Jacobus Tabernaemontanus, Otto Brunfels, Hieronymus Bock, Leonhart Fuchs or Pier Andrea Mattioli appeared with beautiful illustrations by famous artists. The word "Herbarium" – originally relating to collections of dried plants – now also referred to these printed illustrations of plants. Another new type of publication were the so-called pharmacopoeia, authoritative works in which pharmaceutical formulas were fixed and standardised by means of drug and formula lists [for the first time in Nuremberg in 1546]. There were also apothecary manuals, which contained all known "Simplicia" and "Composita" and usually also included a specialist dictionary. They were indispensable sources of information for apothecaries and doctors alike. In the 17th and 18th centuries, these works were constantly revised and adapted to correspond with the latest scientific and medical paradigm shifts. From 1530, the universities at Padua, Bologna, and Pisa had their own chairs of medical botany. This allows one to conclude that the typical cooperation with doctors, which exists today, developed early, particularly in Italy. In the cities of the German imperial cities, most apothecaries were under the control of the authorities who –in keeping with Hohenstaufen tradition – granted them a "privilegium" for a specific city or territory, thus protecting them against the uncontrollable competition of hawkers, miracle doctors, herb gatherers, theriac sellers, and charlatans. Simple people often turned to the monastery apothecaries, where highly valued specific medications with promising names were, to some extent, being developed [Jesuit powder, Capuchin powder, Pulvis Carthusianorum]; not to mention the various different liqueurs.

In the 18th century it was quite common that pharmacist's apprentices were offered lectures in general botany. The academisation of the profession, which complemented medical activities like no other, advanced rapidly. In keeping with the medical edict passed by Frederick Wilhelm I of Prussia [1725], on completion of his apprenticeship and at least seven years as a journeyman, the would-be pharmacist was required to pass a "Processus pharmaceutico-chymicus" at the "Collegium medico-chirurgicum" in Berlin and take a semi-academic examination. Those who wished to set up as pharmacists in small towns could be exempted from the academic examination. The pharmacist's scientific and social standing depended not least on his chosen location.

The 19th century saw a further scientification of pharmacy. Many pharmacists saw themselves as natural scientists – to a far greater extent than did many physicians at the beginning of the century. Talented and ambitious students of the "materia medica", whether their training was "artisanal" or "scientific", now had the opportunity to isolate and artificially produce the active ingredients in traditionally-used plants.

Thus in 1817 Friedrich Wilhelm Sertürner presented morphine in a famous work. Justus von Liebig [1803–1873] rose from being a pharmacist's apprentice in Heppenheim to the position of pharmacy inspector in Hesse, in addition to becoming one of the leading chemists of his age. Thanks to his dedication, pharmacy in Germany was finally academised. It was above all the discovery of alkaloids and glycosides which now influenced the daily lives of pharmacists. While orthodox medicine was in crisis and the Krakow professor Josef Dietl loudly proclaimed its incompetence in 1840 ["therapeutic nihilism"], pharmacology and biochemistry enjoyed a boom. During the second half of the 19th century natural scientific positivism asserted itself within the faculties of medicine. Countless germs were discovered within a relatively short space of time. In close cooperation with physicians, and using the identical methodology, pharmacy and pharmacology were finally promoted to a scientific university subject. The western governments supported this process. The *Société de Pharmacie de Paris*, founded in 1803, saw itself as an elite scientific society, as did the *American Pharmaceutical Association* which was formed in 1852. In many European countries, standardised pharmacopoeia were published on the basis of the latest research, for example, in Germany, the "Pharmacopoea Germanica", the first comprehensive work of this kind in that country. In the old, respected pharmacies, industrially manufactured pharmaceuticals began

4 Pharmacist with mortar in the
  16th century (woodcarving of
  Jost Amman)
5 Stamp for the 750th anniversary of the
  profession of a pharmacist (Deutsche
  Bundespost, 1991)
6 St. Cosmas and St. Damian: patron
  saints of doctor and pharmacist (cover of
  "Feldtbuch der Wundartzney", 1517)
7 Jesus Christ as a pharmacist
  (copperplate print, about 1750)
8 Oil painting of a pharmacist of the
  18th century
9 Pharmacist in the 19th century at his
  place of work

to dominate, whereby some pharmacists, such as Heinrich Merck of Darmstadt, even managed the leap to become major industrialists. The subsequent great wars put the new system to a very special kind of test: The organised storage of huge amounts of pharmaceuticals, vaccines, and various prophylactics made the pharmaceutical industry interesting with regard to military medicine. Mass-produced medication was significantly cheaper than that produced manually, although naturally the pharmacists could no longer vouch for the quality or effectiveness of such products; their job was largely restricted to explaining their effects. In the USA, cheap drugstores were set up, while in Europe "druggists" and herb traders competed with the pharmacists. Interestingly, France differentiated between first and second class pharmacists. In an anti-scientific backlash, both advocates of alternative medicine and charlatans flexed their muscles in the area of pharmacy.

Around the middle of the 20th century, the market became clearer to both patients and physicians: Leave was finally taken from "custom-made" medication. The West German authorities now tried to gain control of the situation by introducing stringent legislation and monitoring the training of pharmacists. The "Obercollegium Medicum et Sanitatis" in Berlin drew up highly rigorous standards in order to regulate the training of pharmacists. The external appearance of the pharmacies developed –

as critics had already bemoaned at the end of the 19th century – into elegant stores. The pharmacist was elevated to become an esteemed member of polite society. Much that was once associated with the pharmacy still is: drugs, medication, herbs, prescriptions, scents, and, above all, well-informed individuals who, in complement to or competition with doctors, offer advice and assistance in case of illness. Such advice is highly valued as medication is still regarded as treacherous: Warnings against side effects are still, indeed increasingly, being made. "Ask your doctor or pharmacist" is a well known slogan. One particular challenge facing pharmacists is the boom in alternative therapies and the astonishingly high level of trust that many people place in non-orthodox medicine. The pharmacist's workplace has undergone a radical change. Modern pharmacies boast a practical design, and the market situation forces the owner to sell products which have only the slenderest connection with health or illness. The trade in industrial pharma products stands to the fore, while the manufacture of remedies and tinctures takes a back seat. Many pharmacies meanwhile resemble health food stores. In terms of quantity, however, the exchange of prescriptions and pharmaceuticals still plays a crucial role. Customers expect pharmacists, who mutated into "academics" in the 19th century, to possess sound scientific knowledge of the various pharma products, their chemical

composition, and their side effects. Pharmacies are also, now more than ever, integrated into the state "health system" all the way through to its mandate as local provider, which cannot be interrupted. Today, as independent businesspeople, many pharmacists feel that they are being led by the nose. Whilst in the golden years of West Germany's economic miracle new pharmacies shot out of the ground like mushrooms and payment for medication from the health insurance funds whose financial scope seemed inexhaustible, presented no problem at all, the current crisis in the health system has also been affecting pharmacies for some time. Their obligations remain but their privileges are dwindling. The international competition from aggressively advertising mail-order pharmacies, online orders, as well as patients and/or customers informing themselves, and the public's increasing disdain for expert advice, are additional sources of pressure. Just like medical practices, hospitals and out-patient clinics, the pharmacy too is facing drastic changes.

SOURCES

Cowen, David L./ Helfand, William H.: Die
Geschichte der Pharmazie in Kunst und
Kultur. Cologne 1991.

Dilg, Peter: Über die Anfänge des mittel-
alterlichen Apothekenwesens. In:
Aumüller, Gerhard ao [ed.]: Der Dienst am
Kranken. Krankenversorgung zwischen
Caritas, Medizin und Ökonomie vom
Mittelalter bis zur Neuzeit. Marburg 2007.
Page 87–99

Gaude, Werner: Die alte Apotheke.
Eine tausendjährige Kulturgeschichte.
Stuttgart 1986.

Richter, Thomas: Apothekerwesen.
In: Gerabek, Werner ao [ed.]: Enzyklopädie
Medizingeschichte. Berlin/New York 2005.
Page 80–86

Schmitz, Rudolf: Geschichte der Pharmazie I. Von den Anfängen bis zum Ausgang
des Mittelalters. Eschborn 1998.

Schmitz, Rudolf: Geschichte der Pharmazie II. Von der Frühen Neuzeit bis zur Gegen-
wart. Eschborn 2005.

The pharmacy in the 21st century
10 DocMorris Apotheke, Munich
  Sales area of a modern pharmacy
11 Pharmacists are trading on the access to the
  internet, as well.
12 Counseling interview in a modern pharmacy
13 Pharmacist in the storage of goods

Every company or organisation has a clear goal: to achieve success in its most diverse dimensions and forms. This success is only achieved, however, if, alongside purely economic success such as increased turnover or profit maximisation, another factor is added: The people who work for a company or organisation need to have a sense of belonging in order to stand up for and work towards a common goal.

The more clearly the goal is formulated, the more unambivalently an institution's purpose is defined, the easier it is to translate this corporate identity into the language of architecture and support it in a targeted way. This applies just as much to pharmacies as to globally operating companies, to religions and churches, to cities and countries. In major companies, the subject of corporate identity has long been a matter of course and, just as is the case for large companies, pharmacies also need to create a corporate identity, a mission and an awareness of purpose, which extends beyond increasing sales figures. An identity which places people's health and health promotion centre-stage and which takes not only monetary success but also the spirit and the soul of pharmacy into account.

Corporate identity doesn't just happen — it has to be developed — to cover every aspect which relates to the company, the organisation, and the pharmacy: corporate behaviour, corporate communications, and corporate design. The market too, with its demands and competitors, together with the products and services, plays a major role in corporate identity.

All of these elements mutually influence one another and stand in an integral relationship with regard to perception and effect. Once defined, however, a corporate identity is not valid for all eternity but requires regular examination and, where necessary, adjustment to changes in framework conditions, attitudes, and values. Of course, one should not lose sight of the company's individuality, its real purpose, and its strengths, simply because a few market parametres have changed. Hasty or premature changes to mission and strategy made in order to achieve short-term success, or in the hope of long-term sustainability, usually have precisely the opposite effect. The corporate identity becomes blurred, the overall image is no longer consistent or authentic.

But it is precisely an authentic, truly lived, and clearly visible corporate identity with which the pharmacy needs to establish itself in the market. Similarly to a brand article, a business such as a pharmacy can likewise anchor itself in the consciousness of patients and customers by means of specific characteristics and features. Consumers are quite willing to accept a higher price for the quality of branded goods because the brand communicates trust and security, and reduces the wish to try out something different or new: This should be the aim of a pharmacy's corporate identity. The identity of the pharmacy as a corporate entity must be so clear that it serves as a benchmark

KLAUS R. BÜRGER

CORPORATE IDENTITY
VISUALISATION OF THE ENTREPRENEURIAL PERSONALITY THROUGH THE ARCHITECTURAL LANGUAGE

for all transactions and activities. It is not only the products that are sold in the pharmacy, but also the people who work there, who need to be able to communicate these standards and values. It is equally important that the building, its location, and its interior design all express and communicate this identity.

The creation and development of a corporate identity is a process in which all of the said sub-aspects should be analysed in detail and with a long-term perspective in mind – from the standpoint of the pharmacy manager, as well as from the standpoints of the employees, the customers, and the patients. Furthermore, the location, competition situation, and demographic factors of the surrounding area need to be integrated into the analysis, because economic success is also essential in securing the pharmacy's long-term existence. As such, the range of over-the-counter products and advisory services being offered must correspond with the needs and demands of the immediate area. The identification of existing and potential target groups gives rise to a range with which the pharmacy can position itself with good prospects of success – provided that there is not already some competitor wooing the same target groups. In consequence, the search for a corporate identity is influenced by internal factors – the strengths and weaknesses upon which the pharmacy and its personnel have a direct impact, as well as those external

aspects – opportunities and risks inherent in the local area – which cannot be controlled directly.

The elements of a corporate identity are also its instruments: behaviour, communication, and design. All three should convey the identity, the entrepreneurial personality, both internally and outwards, creating a sense of belonging amongst the employees and developing a sense of identification amongst clients.

It is the corporate design which is generally first perceived by the outside world. All communication material, from logo to the design of the business stationery, and every individual print or online measure, must have a uniform quality and visual. Visual communication is visible and these visual impressions and judged, consciously and subconsciously, giving rise to either acceptance or rejection. A standardised presence can however also do more: It can enhance the recognition value and influence affective behaviour by increasing the customer's identification with "his pharmacy". A consistent visual appearance also includes a dress code and, not least, the visual design of the pharmacy's own product range. And, finally, one should not forget the interior and external architecture of the dispensary.

An important, but not directly quantifiable component of corporate identity is individual behaviour. On the one hand, the behaviour of the pharmacy manager to his staff with regard to management style, personnel development,

and further training opportunities and in terms of how he deals with criticism, are important. On the other hand, the behaviour of all employees in contact with customers and interested parties, suppliers and service providers, competitors and the public at large, plays an important role – for, after all, the business's inner attitude is being communicated to other people. That applies all the more to health amenities which stand in the service of the people.

Visual appearance and design are components of communication which are in a dialogue with the outside world. When taken together all elements of corporate identity form a harmonious whole, which is positively perceived and accepted by customers and patients: this finally is the business's image.

The architecture and, in particular, the interior design plays an important role in terms of corporate identity. It must not only create spaces, but should and must also reflect the pharmacy's identity – in other words, these spaces too must encourage positive and open behaviour and the willingness of employees and customers to communicate. At the same time, a genius loci must also be shaped, in which customers and patients feel safe, content, and well looked after. Good design has the aim of inspiring people, of making them stay, of arousing wishes, and of stimulating the imagination and ultimately, in terms of shop design's functional aspects, the aim of enhancing people's willingness to buy. This cannot be

1 **Alpin Apotheke am Klinikum, Kempten** Location as the central factor of corporate philosophy – applied to interior design: The Alps are reflected in the colours and materials of the sales area. The panorama picture of the Alps creates a clear cohesion between the interior and the surroundings.

2 **Allmann'sche Apotheke, Biberach** Immediately at the entrance, the logo illustrates the corporate design.

3 **Allmann'sche Apotheke, Biberach** Colours and logo are evident in details throughout the entire dispensary.

achieved in functional rooms in which the product-filled shelves lack emotional character. But where interior design serves its true purpose, it can convey aura and atmosphere, personality and a personal feel to people, thus rendering the corporate identity visible and making it tangible. As such, the design of pharmacies and other health amenities should, in particular, employ creative and sociopsychological expertise to complement the purely technical aspects of interior design.

The elements which interior design can employ are both simple and complex: colour, shape, and material. Each element makes its very own statement and, in its individuality, has an effect on all those who come into contact with it. However, as soon as two or more colours, two or more shapes, two or more materials come together, the statement made by the individual element may no longer be valid, and the elements either mutually strengthen or foil each other: they enter into a dialogue. This interplay is potentialised where all three elements are brought together – just as several different medications taken together may cause pharmaceutical interaction. The interaction profile of colour, shape and material should therefore be professionally coordinated with the corporate identity, so that it corresponds with the corporate philosophy. There, where people feel at home, heal or recover, the interplay between the interior design elements should

be designed with the greatest possible care and circumspection. Depending on the given functional area of the pharmacy – whether over-the-counter sales and cash desk, self-service or over-the-counter display, whether prescriptions or advice – different goals are being pursued with regard to the stimulation of emotions and actions. The potential psychological effects of colours, shapes, and materials must be deployed and combined here in a carefully targeted manner.

The suggestive strength and unconscious effect of colours were known long before Goethe's colour circle. Depending on the intensity of the shade and degree to which they are used, yellow and red, blue and green, or black and white in all their tones and shades can spark off a huge variety of responses. In the health-care area, and thus also in pharmacies, no general statement can be made on whether there are colours which are more likely to encourage recovery and well-being than others. Thus white was traditionally seen as the [non] colour of the healing professions, but has lost ground continually since colour psychology became a fixed feature of the interior design of pharmacies, medical practices, and clinics. The situation is similar with regard to the selection of shapes and materials. Curves always appear softer than sharp edges and are also employed at a superordinate level in pharmacies: Wherever the space of the dispensary permits, bends and

curves can be used to steer the paths of customers and patients. The psychology of paths can be applied, people's automatic tendency to veer to the right can be taken into account, and customers can be unconsciously steered to the self-service section if there is sufficient space in the sales area. The choice of suitable materials for a pharmacy is made in light of functionality and aesthetics. Where robustness and durability are required, they must also be guaranteed. For, just as a pharmacy's corporate identity is built to last, equally, the interior design of the pharmacy should not be subject to frequent change or, even worse, display signs of wear and tear. A corporate identity is not a fashion statement and its visual must also communicate constant sustainability and tangible authenticity. If the personality of the pharmacy is best expressed in a glowing shade of orange then the communication of this personality can outlive any trend using precisely this colour, or possibly only using it as a highlight, in the pharmacy.

Fashion consciousness however is no contradiction to a corporate identity geared to the long term. A good corporate identity can also be implemented by means of effective, topical advertising strategies and measures. This is a question of nuances, details – it is not about the pharmacy as a whole. It should be made clear here, that "measures" refers not just to the design of eye-catching posters and advertisements. Rather, it is the choice of product range, the type and way in which goods are placed, and the question of

whether customers are addressed in a loud or quiet manner – all elements which are just as important as the consistent use of the corporate design. Even the training of employees with regard to providing expert advice during special, target group-oriented campaigns or in the areas of starting conversation, question techniques or handling objections, is an element of customer-oriented corporate identity.

The interior design of a pharmacy is more than the harmonious composition of various functional areas to create a pretty dispensary, because an "attractive" pharmacy is either the expression of a corporate culture or it is an empty façade – and today's customers and patients are well able to differentiate between exactly the two.

SOURCES

Antonoff, Roman: CI-Report 13. Darmstadt 2004.

Bürger, Klaus R.: Apothekenarchitektur – funktionsgerecht & ästhetisch. In: Offprint Anzag Magazin. Frankfurt/Main 1997.

Damaschke, Sabine/Scheffer, Bernadette: Apotheken. Planen, Gestalten und Einrichten. Leinfelden-Echterdingen 2000.

Kreft, Wilhelm: Ladenplanung. Merchandising – Architektur. Strategie für Verkaufsräume: Gestaltungs-Grundlagen, Erlebnis-Inszenierungen, Kundenleitweg, Planungen. Leinfelden-Echterdingen 1993 .

Weis , H. C.: Marketing. Ludwigshafen 1997.

4 **Schiller Apotheke, Heidenheim**
White is no longer the rule of thumb when designing healthcare amenities: rich red …

5 **Michaels Apotheke, Winterbach**
… dark blue,

6 **Adler Apotheke, Göppingen**
… delicate green,

7 **Hardt Apotheke, Hambrücken**
… restrained natural shades

8 **Burg Apotheke, Grefrath-Oedt**
Customer orientation in loving detail: flowers at the cash desk

9 **Aurelia Apotheke, Baden-Baden**
Beautifully staged dispensary in a city of culture

10 **Alte Apotheke, Scheven**
An awareness of tradition is demonstrated all the way through to lounge and consulting room, old values with a modern twist.

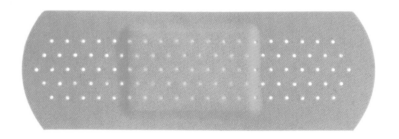

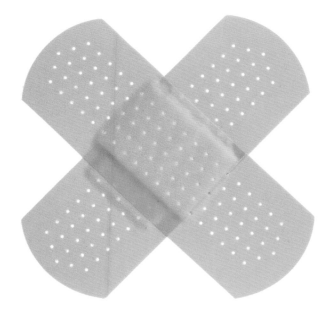
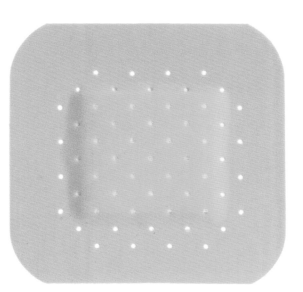

When it comes to designing healthcare amenities, special sensitivity is required. This principle applies perhaps even more with regard to the interior design of pharmacies. To a greater extent than medical practices or clinics, pharmacies have to walk a thin line between the needs of ill people, those individuals who wish to preserve their health, and the economic requirements and necessities of retail trade.

On the one hand, the pharmacist's self-image demands that a place of recovery, healing, and care be created using all means available, including those of interior design. On the other hand, as a businessman the pharmacist is subject to the economic necessities of achieving turnover and making a profit, in order to secure and expand his business over the long term – and this too must be done using all available means. Not least, he must create a pleasant working atmosphere, so that the employees in both the sales area and the function rooms have the opportunity to develop their performance, are more willing to perform, and enter into open communication both with customers and each other.

Irrespective of whether the project in hand is a new construction or a redesign, there are countless ways of combining the elements of interior design. The walls, ceilings, and floors alone offer a wide spectrum of different choices. Once a wall has been immovably fixed in place, it can only be perceived differently by means of

colour. Different shades of colour, or patterns to add depth, are the simplest option; more complicated options, in construction terms, would be breaking through the solid material by inserting glass, or by creating openings to serve as viewing windows, sources of light or extra shelf space.

Colouring plays an important role in designing floors and ceilings as the choice of a light or dark colour has a major influence on subconscious perception: A dark floor communicates an earthed position, firm standing, and a strong foothold. In contrast, a light floor conveys weightlessness. With regard to ceilings, light tones can increase and darker shades reduce the perceived height of a room. As an alternative, both floors and ceilings can use graphic or constructional elements. Thus, for example, the ceiling can be used to continue an artistic or creative wall design – or lighting can be integrated into the ceiling design.

Light and architecture – two elements which must be linked together in order to achieve a positive effect. It is important that, right from the start, the element of light is accorded its true importance in the concept and not simply "tacked on" once the shop is complete. Light in interior design means not only illumination with artificial light but also plans in natural light – daylight: It is always the basis and starting point of all lighting considerations and should, wherever available, always be integrated into the design. Nonetheless, there is scarcely any sales area or pharmacy which can manage without artificial light. For this reason,

KLAUS R. BÜRGER

DESIGN
FUNCTIONALITY, SHAPING, SENSITIVITY

artificial light should be seen and deployed as a variant and expansion of the natural light, because "natural" lighting creates a sense of confidence and comfort in the visitor.

In order to create a lighting atmosphere which appears natural, shadow is also necessary: Alongside lighter areas, there must also be darker ones because completely shadow-free illumination lacks differentiation, paradoxically appearing somewhat lifeless and thus counterproductive. Light makes the sales area visible. How the sales area should be made visible to the eye is important for the shop planning. In terms of lighting, there are three main areas in each of which the degree of illumination should vary:

General lighting

General lighting should provide a technical balance for the absence of daylight. In the retail trade, it is normal to reduce general lighting and, in its place, use a greater number of illumination highlights the more exclusive and expensive the goods on offer are. Translated to the pharmacy, a dispensary with an upmarket range can certainly use general lighting with a low lux level. Alongside well-balanced general lighting, different spots integrated into the ceiling and arranged at regular intervals can provide a seamless transition to area lighting, thus supporting the task of guiding the customer's path.

Area lighting

Luminaires and type of light are adapted to the differing requirements in the various areas of the sales room. Generally speaking, the differences here are created by light colour.

Accent lighting

Highlighting is provided by additional lights, individual luminaires and focused light from single spots. Colour changes, stark light contrasts, unusual lighting angles or artistically sculptural lighting are tools with which the customer's attention may be influenced with light. When highlighting individual items or areas, it is important that the luminosity be significantly higher than that of the general lighting. A mixture of these three types of lighting creates an integrated lighting design. And variety is also important: Using a mix of stimulating and relaxing light elements promotes the customer's attention and concentration. As the Brazilian theologian Dom Hélder Pessoa Câmara said: "The light that falls on things transforms them." The colours chosen for floor, ceiling, walls, and furnishings are fundamental to the design of a room's atmosphere. As such, the correct reproduction of the chosen colours under artificial light is absolutely essential. Different luminaires have different colour reproduction properties, that means different colour effects which cause the light on coloured surfaces or objects to be seen differently.

Deciding on colour is the next element in an integrated overall design. The subconscious perception and effects of colours were already examined in some depth by Goethe in 1791. Meanwhile, colour has become an elementary component, not only in interior design and advertising psychology but also, in particular, in shop design: How can customers be put into the right mood to enter a business, feel at home, or buy a product? Red to arouse attention; yellow to generate a good mood; green for harmony; blue for tranquillity. However, all of these colours together, alongside, beneath or on top of each other tend to have the opposite effect. None of the individual colours can work properly, none can effectively develop its influence on people and its mood. It is not only in retail but also often in the pharmacy that one becomes aware – sometimes painfully so – of this. Self-service and over-the-counter goods display dozens of differently coloured packages, flashing shelf stoppers and colourful price signs; the eyes are also assaulted by additional stands for leaflets, brochures, ceiling hangers, decorative pillars, and floor mats. However, the pharmacy is meant to be a place for health and not a centre for psychological advertising messages. Carefully planned details can easily create a different, calmer atmosphere. The full strength of a colour however only becomes evident when one specific shade is employed, possibly linked with a second colour for highlighting and contrast. "Stick to the essentials" should be the maxim when it comes to

1 **Kreuz-Apotheke, Hanover**
The material and colour dialogue creates a deliberate tension and promotes the desired guidance of the customer.

2 **Schwanen Apotheke, Stuttgart**
Dark shades for the floor area create a sense of safety and being well looked after in the customer and represent a deliberate counterbalance to the room's height.

3 **Alpin Apotheke am Klinikum, Kempten** Effective yet discreet product presentation, achieved by reducing material, mass, and colour. The change from dark flooring in the self-service area to light flooring in the over-the-counter product area subconsciously conveys a boundary to the customer.

the further design of the space, particularly the sales area, because particularly in pharmacies, the points of sale [POS] , shelves, gondola displays, and rummage tables are essential furnishings, which have to fit in harmoniously with the overall image. Provided that there is adequate floor space, customers can also be guided specifically to the self-service products by means of room dividers and gondola shelves, something which is of distinct advantage to pharmacies with a high number of casual customers. In this regard the customer should ideally be guided past as many product groups as possible, through to the POS, as it is generally assumed that the customer should see as many products as possible which entice him to make a purchase. This may certainly be the case for certain sectors but those who recall the works of Andreas Gursky will also be aware that mass and quantity do not necessarily have a positive effect on the individual's sense of well-being. Increasing numbers of people feel that they are being more or less "crushed" by the weight of choice in department stores, supermarkets, and pharmacies.

Reducing the information overload by deliberately cutting back the number of goods on offer means that the pharmacy customer is able to absorb more. Sensible interior design limits information overload by reflecting the material and colour language of the interior in the material and colour language of the entire space:

Materials which, in their final form, do not grab the attention and which only make their statement subconsciously, are perfect for self-service shelves, given that the product itself then becomes the focus of interest, without appearing loud or obtrusive. Alternatively, the dialogue between colour, shape, and material can also be used in a targeted manner, for example in designing the POS, in order to emphasise the desired statement made by the interior design, to create a tension, and to stimulate or calm both customer and employee. The selection of the right colour combination, the influence of daylight or artificial light on the shade and saturation, the interplay of material and shape, colour and light should be understood and implemented by the designer as a single whole.

Where the focus of the concept is on the pharmacy as a centre of competence, it must convey this uniformly and coherently in all aspects at first glance because the pharmacy customer is – both consciously and subconsciously – in a position to perceive and evaluate the dispensing area as an expression of the corporate culture and pharmacy philosophy.

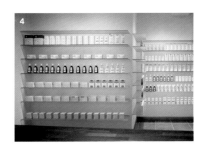

SOURCES

Bürger, Klaus R.: Apothekenarchitektur – funktionsgerecht & ästhetisch. In: Offprint Anzag Magazin. Frankfurt/Main 1997.

Damaschke, Sabine/Scheffer, Bernadette: Apotheken. Planen, Gestalten und Einrichten. Leinfelden-Echterdingen 2000.

Kreft, Wilhelm: Ladenplanung. Merchandising – Architektur. Strategie für Verkaufsräume: Gestaltungs-Grundlagen, Erlebnis-Inszenierungen, Kundenleitweg, Planungen. Leinfelden-Echterdingen 1993.

4 **Apotheke am Klemensplatz, Düsseldorf** By using restrained colour and material language, the product is automatically placed centre-stage.

5 **Tilly Apotheke, Stadtlohn** The colour and material of the furnishings are reflected in the overall space concept and create a calming atmosphere.

6 **Arnica Apotheke, Marktoberdorf** The design principles used in the sales area are optimally repeated in the function rooms as well.

7 **Rathaus Apotheke, Frankfurt/Main** Floor-embedded spots of light serving as guides create a discreet distance.

8 **Fleming Apotheke, Dortmund** Logical customer path: In keeping with the automatic veer to the right, the path goes past the self-service area, in-depth customer service at the table, and finally to the queue at the POS.

9 **Marien Apotheke, Eriskirch** Reinforcement of the automatic veer to the right by using curved walls in the self-service area.

The potential owners or leaseholders of the pharmacy and all of those involved in the planning, that means architects and interior designers, and possibly artists, engineers, and suppliers, must engage very closely with the operational and constructional principles of planning, whether new construction, expansion or redesign, if they wish to create what is by today's standards a high-performing, economically viable, customer-friendly and well-designed pharmacy. The following sections provide information on planning, construction, and furnishing.

TYPES OF PHARMACY

According to the *Federal Union of German Associations of Pharmacists* (ABDA), there are 21,570 pharmacies[1] in Germany. Depending on how one looks at them, they may be divided into the following categories:

CLASSIFICATION BY SIZE | A rough observation leads to classification into small, medium-sized and large pharmacies. Precise definition of the respective sizes is provided in the "Usable areas" section.

CLASSIFICATION BY LOCATION | Because the services provided often vary, a differentiation is made between urban pharmacies and rural pharmacies.

CLASSIFICATION BY NEIGHBOURHOOD | For both customers and pharmacy it is economically important to be close to other businesses or, better still, to be in the direct vicinity of other businesses in the form of a pharmacy within a department store. The greatest benefits accrue to the pharmacy in a healthcare facility, because the definition of a need and its satisfaction are in the same premises.

CLASSIFICATION BY TYPE OF SALE | A differentiation should be made between physical pharmacies which sell their products to customers locally and mail-order pharmacies which, while retaining the functions of a physical pharmacy have a special licence and are primarily focused on dispatching goods to fulfil customer orders.

CLASSIFICATION IN ACCORDANCE WITH ABDA | The vast majority are main or standalone pharmacies [with operating licence] – just under eleven percent being chain pharmacies.

CLASSIFICATION PURSUANT TO THE "ORDINANCE GOVERNING THE OPERATION OF PHARMACIES" [APOTHEKEN-BETRIEBSORDNUNG: APBETRO[2]] | Here a differentiation is made between public pharmacies, hospital-supplying pharmacies, branch and emergency pharmacies, and hospital pharmacies.

CLASSIFICATION BASED ON DEVELOPMENT OF MARKETING | A very recent differentiation, whose importance will certainly increase in future, is that

FRANZ LABRYGA

PRINCIPLES OF PLANNING
PHARMACIES

between premium pharmacies which feature high product quality and offer advice and care to customers, and discount pharmacies, who primarily advertise with bargain prices, aim for high product turnover, and largely dispense with service and customer advice. In the present work, only the first three categories are applied.

LEGISLATION, ORDINANCES, AND OTHER REGULATIONS

Special regulations apply to the construction of pharmacies, the observance of which is of crucial importance, particularly with regard to averting danger from customers and employees. [Fig. 1, 2]

APBETRO

This ordinance passed on 26 September 1995 [revised on 20 July 2007] regulates the operation of pharmacies and the supply of medication to the public. It is rooted in article 21 of the "Pharmacy Act" [Gesetz über das Apothekenwesen[3]], which forms the basis for the establishment of all pharmacies in Germany. In both main sections of the APBETRO employee prerequisites, requirements with regard to the manufacture, storage, and designation of medications, and the size and furnishing of the business premises are regulated. Individual details are specified in the relevant sections of the planning principles.

Other requirements

The text of the APBETRO also draws attention to other legal requirements to be fulfilled for the operation of a pharmacy:
- German Pharmacy Act [Gesetz über das Apothekenwesen/Apothekengesetz]
- German Medicines Act [Gesetz über den Verkehr mit Arzneimitteln/Arzneimittelgesetz]
- Medical Products User Regulations [Medizinprodukte-Betreiberverordnung]
- Ordinance on Medical Devices Vigilance [Medizinprodukte-Sicherheitsplanverordnung]
- Business Trading Hours Act [Ladenschlussgesetz]

The guideline published by the *Robert Koch Institute* "Hygiene requirements for the functional and constructional design and operation of in-hospital and hospital-supplying pharmacies"[4], also applies to other pharmacies with similar duties. The following details are taken from a list by Damaschke and Scheffer[5] of further regulations to be observed when setting up a pharmacy:

LAWS
- Narcotics Act [Betäubungsmittelgesetz]
- Medicinal Advertising Act [Heilmittelwerberecht]
- Working Hours Act [Arbeitszeitgesetz]
- Young Persons' Employment Act [Jugendarbeitsschutzgesetz]

- Maternity Protection Act [Mutterschutzgesetz]
- Employee Protection Act [Beschäftigtenschutzgesetz]

ORDINANCES, REGULATIONS, AND GUIDELINES
- General Administrative Regulation on the Implementation of the Medicines Act [Allgemeine Verwaltungsvorschrift zur Durchführung des Arzneimittelgesetzes]
- Guideline for Awarding Supplier Licences [Richtlinie für die Erteilung der Genehmigung von Versorgungsverträgen]
- Official Approval and Inspection of Pharmacies [Amtliche Abnahme und Besichtigung von Apotheken]
- Granting of Operating Licence [Erteilung der Betriebserlaubnis]
- Hazardous Materials Ordinance [Gefahrstoffverordnung]
- Flammable Liquids Ordinance [Verordnung über brennbare Flüssigkeiten]
- Chemicals Ban Ordinance [Chemikalienverbotsverordnung]
- Narcotics Prescription Ordinance [Betäubungsmittel-Verschreibungsverordnung]
- Guidelines | Good Manufacturing Practices
- Federal Pharmacists' Code – BAPO [Bundesapothekerordnung]
- Administrative and Professional Guidelines [Verwaltungs- und Berufsgenossenschaftliche Vorschriften]
- Accident Prevention Regulations of the Statutory

1

1 Architect in planning phase examining compliance with regulations, Sketch: Hartmann

Insurance Association for Non-State Health Services and Welfare Work [Unfallverhütungsvorschriften der Berufsgenossenschaft für Gesundheitsdienst und Wohlfahrtspflege]
– Workplace Ordinance [Arbeitsstättenverordnung]
– German Standards Regulations [DIN-Vorschriften]
– Federal State Construction Ordinances [Landesbauordnungen]
– Trade, Commerce, and Industry Regulation Act [Gewerbeordnung]
– Labelling Regulations [Kennzeichenvorschriften]
– Professional Code of the Pharmacists' Chamber [Berufsordnung der Apothekenkammer]
– Competition Law [Wettbewerbsrecht]

In case of need, reference will be made in the following explanations to the regulations mentioned above.

DATA REQUIRED FOR OPERATION

The implementation of a planning idea starts with the consideration of the establishment's future operations. On this basis construction is later undertaken.

The following is an explanation of the operating requirements which are important for pharmacies:

Catchment area

One indicator of a pharmacy's importance and the level of its profile is the size of the catchment area from which the majority of its customers come. Some pharmacies also have a large catchment area because the population density, for example in rural areas, is relatively low. Where customers have to travel a long way to the pharmacy, whether on foot, with public transport, or by car, the pharmacist should consider what amenities he would like to offer them. He should consider providing seating and rest areas, particularly for old or disabled people, as well as refreshment in the shape of a mineral water dispenser, and a WC. The impact of demographic structure and type of customer within the catchment area on the pharmacy's economic development should not be underestimated. Successful pharmacies integrate this data when planning their sales strategies.

Location

The considerations which apply when choosing a good home also apply to pharmacies. The top three criteria are location, location, location. It is therefore urgently recommended that before any detailed planning is made, a thorough location analysis be undertaken, in order to find out the best location for the future pharmacy. The following locations are advantageous:
– locations with a high number of people passing by, whether on main roads, in pedestrian zones or in houses with highly varied frequency of passers-by, such as department stores or shopping centres, railway stations or airports
– locations in or close to healthcare facilities where medications are prescribed: group medical practices or health centres, the practices of GPs or specialist physicians, gymnastic and massage practices, care centres, podiatry clinics, beauty parlours or spas.
The following locations are a disadvantage:
– locations which are too close to existing pharmacies, except where level of footfall permits such competition and that this competitive situation even proves to be healthy
– locations with no connection to the local transport network: in general, locations which are more than 200 metres from a public transport stop are unsuitable.

Arrangement of products

The original meaning of the word "apothecary" [storehouse] still remains valid to some extent today. As in times past, storage still plays an essential role, although a quite different one to before.

DELIVERY OF GOODS | Goods for the pharmacy usually arrive at regular intervals, conveniently delivered in transport containers or on pallets via a dedicated route to the stockroom, which is practically located at ground floor level or in a basement accessible by elevator. In larger pharmacies, a room for receiving the goods comes before the stockroom itself; where the pharmacy itself consigns a lot of goods, it makes sense to have a space or room for dispatching goods.

NUMBER OF ARTICLES IN STOCK | To be precise, this refers to the number of different types of article and the number of units of the individual types which are constantly in stock at the pharmacy. A large number of medicines are ordered as required. Depending on the distance from the distributing warehouse, items can mostly be handed over to the customer within a few hours or on the following day.

STOCK TURNOVER | The size of a stockroom depends not only on the type and number of medicines constantly in stock, but also on how fast the stock is turned over. Once a pharmacist has agreed fast and reliable delivery with suppliers, storage areas can be reduced in size accordingly. The constantly increasing differentiation in the choice of goods available in recent years often forces existing pharmacies to enter into such agreements. However, in newly established pharmacies, this method can be useful. For pharmacies in rural areas, frequent deliveries may be more difficult to arrange because of the greater distances involved.

SIZE AND TYPE OF STOCKROOM | The determining factors for the size of the stockroom are the number of packaged goods kept in stock,

the height of the stockrooms, and the type of storage. There are two different types of stockroom:

– ABC storage [alphabetical storage] | The items are arranged in alphabetical order. This method of storage makes it easier to find medicines and, because there is barely any technical dependency, permits a high level of supply security.
– chaotic storage | The items are arranged according to how fast they sell and the available storage capacity. This method of storage requires a good data processing system and the entry and dispensing of medicines needs to be automated. Alongside only a low rate of error in ordering, the space saved is a major advantage. Increasingly, pharmacies are using automated stockrooms, which are available in semi-automatic or fully automatic form. A thorough cost-benefit analysis should be carried out before deciding on which type of storage to use. Under special circumstances, pharmacies also have an emergency stockroom specially for those medicines which are most urgently required in emergencies.

GOODS TRANSPORT | Items may be transported by trolley or using automated systems in the shape of pneumatic delivery, conveyor belts, spindle-shaped chutes or, in large pharmacies such as those in hospitals, box-type conveyor systems which transport the ordered items across longer

distances to their various destinations. Deciding which method to choose largely depends on local conditions and the performance level required. Owing to the not insignificant investment and operating costs for automated transport systems, a thorough analysis should be carried out before an automated stockroom is set up.

Waste disposal
Waste disposal is subject to the requirements laid down by the *Federal Ministry of the Environment*. Waste occurring in pharmacies in usually collected at regular intervals by waste management companies. Special attention is given to toxins, including medicines as well as organic and inorganic chemicals, and expired narcotics. The disposal of them is regulated by the Narcotics Act. Special rules apply to medicines which are out of date: They are either collected and disposed of by wholesalers, or the pharmacies are required to organise their disposal themselves.

In-house manufacture
A total of six clauses of the APBETRO concern themselves with the in-house manufacture and examination of medicines in pharmacies. Apart from general regulations on management and examination [§ 6], requirements with regard to formulation [§ 7], small scale production [§ 8], large-scale production [§ 9], examination and approval of medicines [§ 10], and the constituent ingredients [§ 11] must also be met. In light of the ever growing

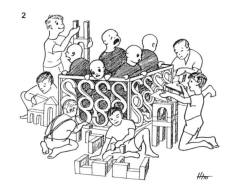

2 "Special regulations apply to the construction of pharmacies, the observance of which is of crucial importance, particularly with regard to averting danger from customers and employees." Sketch: Hartmann

spread of industrially produced finished products, the present level of in-house manufacture will probably decrease considerably in future.

Specialist advice

The main duty of the pharmacy sales staff is to provide customers with specialist advice. This is provided in a discreet way. It may also include the query as to whether the customer has understood everything he has been told. The customers' experiences in this regard form the core of their judgment, which may be crucial to the pharmacy's survival. Advisory services have expanded significantly in recent years; today they are regularly assisted by the latest reference material and the internet.

Special services

In view of the worsening of the market situation in recent times due to increased competition and reduced purchasing power, pharmacists have continually expanded their range of services.

Using imagination and creativity, numerous new services have been created which help to increase attractiveness. There are five areas in which pharmacies have become active:

EXPANSION OF THE PRODUCT RANGE
– expansion of the range in the area of "typical pharmacy products"
– preparation of individual formulations for teas, creams, capsules and cosmetic products
– inclusion of products typically sold in medical supplies stores
– manufacture of cytostatics

EXPANSION OF ADVISORY SERVICES
– allergy advice
– medicinal tolerance check
– skincare
– nutrition and dietary advice
– endocrinological advice
– homoeopathic advice
– babycare
– incontinency advice
– vaccination advice
– travel advice and mediation, particularly for long-haul trips
– medical and scientific research

PERFORMING HEALTHCARE TASKS
– measuring blood pressure, uric acid, blood sugar, and cholesterol
– measuring weight
– measuring vein pressure
– incontinence and stoma care
– body structure analysis
– skin analysis
– facial analysis
– podiatry
– massage
– pregnancy testing
– fitting for compression tights

– cosmetic treatments
– spa/fitness treatments

EXPANSION OF SERVICES
– information by e-mail
– collection of prescriptions
– introduction of a customer card
– home deliveries of medicines
– obtaining quotations from the health insurance funds
– taking orders by telephone, telefax, and e-mail
– supplying health facilities
– automatic fee calculations
– import and export of medicines
– lending baby scales
– organising self-help groups
– setting up a health café

ORGANISATION OF COURSES AND SEMINARS
– courses for healthy eating
– walking courses
– yoga courses
– fasting weeks
– lectures on clinical pictures
– readings on subjects which promote health
– seminars on dietetics and healthy eating

The planner should be aware of the type and scope of such special services, as these activities will have an impact on the type and number of rooms required and their floor areas.

Sale of pharmacy products

In economic terms, the pharmacy's main goal is to sell goods in an efficient way, achieving high turnover, and increasing profit. Ultimately, all efforts are made to achieve this goal [Fig. 3–5]. A lastingly effective corporate philosophy [corporate identity] means that while doing this, great attention is paid to the customer's well-being.

Supplying third parties

It is beneficial to a pharmacy's balance sheet if it can manage to constantly deliver pharmacy products to one or more healthcare facilities. These include, for example, sheltered housing, old people's homes, homes for the disabled, medical practices and group practices, medical supply centres, and hospitals. Where such deliveries are constant, because of the increased turnover of goods, the pharmacy requires both a larger stockroom, but also areas for receiving goods and, depending on the type of consignment, for packaging, inventory management, and dispatch. In any event, adequate space for vehicles with incoming and outbound goods is required in front of the pharmacy [Fig. 6–8].

Personnel deployment

Clauses 2, 3, and 28 of the APBETRO regulate pharmacy personnel. A pharmacy is required to have a manager as well as the necessary pharmaceutical and non-pharmaceutical staff. The pharmaceutical personnel includes the pharmacist, pharmaceutical technical assistants, pharmacist's assistants, pharmacy technicians, pharmaceutical assistants, and the respective trainees; the non-pharmaceutical personnel includes pharmacy assistants, skilled pharmacy staff, and commercial staff with pharmaceutical training. In a pharmacy that is integrated in a hospital, this very clearly defined range of personnel corresponds with the type and performance structure of the hospital. For other pharmacies, the ordinance specifies that the criterion for personnel requirements is that a properly operating business structure be guaranteed.

The type and, above all, number of staff are crucial factors in determining the size of usable areas in service rooms, staff rooms, and also in changing rooms.

Operating costs

Ultimately all operational considerations with regard to organising a customer-friendly and well-performing pharmacy have the aim of keeping whole the operating costs in reasonable check.

Firstly, there are the personnel costs which comprise around 70 percent of total costs. Careful thought should therefore be given to the deployment of pharmaceutical and non-pharmaceutical personnel. A basic prerequisite for economic staffing is the organisation of optimised workflows for the pharmacy's main work processes. With regard to material costs too, which are largely made up of energy costs, costs for consumables, the cost of the premises, and advertising costs, efficient deployment is necessary in order to achieve a favourable operating result.

DATA REQUIRED FOR CONSTRUCTION

Taking the specified operational data into account, the data required for construction can now be established and collated. The two data packages form the basis for further activities and decisions with regard to the layout and design of the pharmacy.

Urban development requirements

BUILDING PLOT | In the case of a new construction being planned, when choosing a building plot, both the square metre price as well as the size, and the existing building regulation must be taken into account. A farsighted purchaser will ensure that the size of the plot allows for later expansion, and thus for the potential development of the pharmacy itself.

TRANSPORT CONNECTIONS | Good accessibility has a crucial influence on whether or not a pharmacy can survive. This applies in particular for clients who come to the pharmacy on foot, as well as to those who are also reliant on public transport with nearby stops.

3-5 Sale of pharmacy products in a modern pharmacy.
6-8 DocMorris Apotheke, Munich
Arrangement of products

PRESERVATION ORDERS | An old pharmacy which is of outstanding architectural design and therefore listed is a gem, for both the owner and the customers, who enjoy visiting for this quality alone. Usually, however, the authorities impose strict conditions on any construction work, so that it is very difficult to make alterations and the pharmacy must often manage with functional shortcomings.

Measures to preserve the building's substance can also be very expensive. Consolation prizes exist in the shape of occasional public funding, or financial support granted by sponsors to preserve such a historic legacy.

Usable areas

Apart from the public area, the construction area and the technical functional area, the usable area is the most important type of area in terms of a building's breakdown of gross area as laid down in DIN 277[6]. While the first three types of area are the same in every type of building, the usable area – as the name suggests – gives an insight into its project-specific use. It is therefore the most powerful key indicator in a floor plan.

Since size is one of the main differentiating features of pharmacies, the respective usable areas are used for differentiation. With regard to the examples presented in this book, and with regard to existing development trends, the following applies:

– pharmacies with usable areas of up to 175 sqm: small pharmacies
– pharmacies with usable areas of 176 to 350 sqm: medium-sized pharmacies
– pharmacies with usable areas of over 350 sqm: large pharmacies

Space allocation plan

In light of the previous explanations, it becomes clear that only the usable areas can be recorded in the space allocation plans required for planning pharmacies. All other areas, [public, technical functional, and construction areas] are only defined during the drafting phase.

The rooms should be specified by type and size in the space allocation plans. The following are useful indicators with regard to planning the illumination of rooms:
○ daylight required
◉ daylight desired
● daylight not required

DIN 13080 "Division of Hospitals into Functional Areas and Functional Sections"[7], a standard which has now been successfully applied in hospital planning for over 20 years, even beyond Germany's borders, contains a recommendation on the breakdown of space allocation plans. This states that rooms should be divided into four groups:
– main rooms
– auxiliary rooms

– connecting rooms
– staff rooms

The planner may decide whether he wishes to break down his space allocation plan in this way, or whether he prefers to use the breakdown by functional groups described in the following section. For the sake of consistency, this book uses functional groups throughout.

Breakdown into functional groups

In planning a pharmacy, a large number of different types of room need to be considered. In order to reduce this large number, some rooms with similar purposes are included under the same heading, for example stockrooms for infusions, drugs or tea are classified under "special storage". In planning terms it has proven practical to allocate the around 40 rooms which remain after the standardisation of designations, into specific room units.

Since, compared with hospitals, the room units in a pharmacy are relatively small, the classification of "functional group" has been introduced. Similar to the method used in DIN 13080, colour markers are used, which considerably ease the tasks of collating the floor plan arrangements and of analysing and comparing plans. The eight functional groups briefly outlined below are not present in every pharmacy, but depend rather on the type of pharmacy and its performance profile.

CUSTOMER ROOMS | The rooms allocated to this functional group comprise the dispensary which forms the heart of the pharmacy, with facilities for self-service and counter sales and the cash desk. In general, it is only in medium-sized and large pharmacies that special purpose rooms, a reception area, a waiting room, a play area for children, a WC, one or more consulting rooms, an intensive consultancy room, a treatment room, and a beauty treatment room are foreseen. In any event, the customer rooms should include a night service counter and, where pharmacies are suitably located in transport terms, a drive-in counter. The customer room functional group is marked in yellow in floor plans.

BUSINESS ROOMS | It is frequently the case that business rooms, with the exception of the stockroom, are classified as all rooms which are not customer rooms. For better differentiation, however, the term is more closely defined here. Such rooms include those rooms which are essential to the fulfilment of core business: the alphabetically-organised stockroom, one or more workplaces, prescription room, and a lab. Cost-cutting solutions combine the prescription room and lab in a single room. This functional group is marked in red.

SPECIAL PURPOSE ROOMS | This functional group is usually only present in large pharmacies. Such rooms have special functions, for example a cytostatics room with sluice, a parenterals room, and a physical stockroom. The rarely encountered herb garden is also included in this group. This functional group is marked in pink.

ADMINISTRATIVE ROOMS | This relatively small functional group comprises the rooms required for the administration of the pharmacy. These primarily include one or more offices and, in large pharmacies, a separate room for purchasing and orders, a room for collections, and an archive. Administrative rooms are marked in floor plans in green.

SERVICE AND STAFF ROOMS | This functional group comprises those rooms which are required for the pharmacy manager's duties, for staff use, and for sanitary purposes, and include service rooms, the night service room, the staff rooms with pantry, and the sanitary rooms, that means changing rooms, showers, and WCs. In terms of making savings, it is possible to combine staff room with night service room or with the pantry. Very occasionally there are libraries, also used as consulting rooms, and a separate room for sales to staff. These service and staff rooms are marked in orange.

SUPPLY AND WASTE DISPOSAL ROOMS | The rooms required by the pharmacy for supply and waste disposal purposes largely comprise the storage areas. In larger establishments there are also rooms for incoming goods, special storage, an emergency depot, and an order room for the packaging and dispatch of goods. The cleaning room and waste disposal room also belong to this functional group. Supply and waste disposal rooms are marked in brown.

TRAINING ROOMS | Rooms for the manifold education of customers and staff are still rare. These are lecture, teaching, and seminar rooms, also functioning as multi-purpose rooms, which may also serve as reserve space for future expansion. Training rooms are subsequently marked in violet.

PLANT ROOMS | Dedicated rooms are required in larger pharmacies for the installation of technical systems. These are technical rooms and shafts for electrical and air conditioning systems, as well as for pneumatic delivery tubes and transport facilities in automated warehouses. This type of room is marked in floor plans in blue.

Individual rooms
Of the around 40 standard rooms in a pharmacy, one part largely comprises rooms for normal use. These include all rooms belonging to the functional groups of administrative rooms, service and social rooms, some of the supply and waste disposal rooms, as well as the training rooms. In the following text, indications of specific characteristics are sufficient. The remaining rooms characteristic of pharmacies should be considered

a little more closely. Detailed descriptions of the requirements for fitting out and furnishing these rooms are contained in the publications "Apotheken" by Damaschke and Scheffer, and "Apothekenbesichtigung" by Spegg[8].

Generally it is the case that the following rooms do not necessarily need to be usable areas completely surrounded by walls. They may often be open or, in case, semi-open areas, so that as transparent an effect as possible is created overall.

DISPENSARY | The largest and most important room in the pharmacy is the dispensary. Today, this room is not only used to dispense medicines but to also fulfil the other duties specified in the APBETRO, that means to provide information and advice.

In order to properly perform these duties, different areas have formed within the greater space, which break it down and give it its characteristic feel. Customers entering the pharmacy first see the self-service shelves; these contain what is actually the secondary range. In accordance with the APBETRO, these are pharmacy-typical products. The customer may select these items himself and purchase them. Customers do not have access to the goods sold over-the-counter. These are shelves containing prescription-only medicines, or for which the pharmacist's advice is required. At the heart of the dispensary is the large sales counter [POS], or as are increasingly being seen, smaller, individual POS, which are described in more detail in the chapter "Design Elements". It is possible to create a lastingly pleasant impression on the customer by offering him services such as fresh water or other drinks, seating, a place to hang his coat, or the opportunity to check his precise weight.

SPECIAL PURPOSE ROOMS | Although the APBETRO specifies that the spread of self-service products should not play a superordinate role to or obstruct the pharmacy's primary objective of dispensing medicine, the self-service range also expands for economic reasons. It is therefore not surprising that the customer area in new pharmacies is increasing in size, and that dispensaries are thus becoming larger. Special purpose areas can be counted as part of the dispensary or listed separately because of their special status. It is convenient for customers if product groups are clearly organised into main strategic selling areas, for example cosmetics, dental care, children, seniors, intimate hygiene, nutrition, sport, and holiday.

PLAY AREA FOR CHILDREN | A stroll through a pharmacy full of tempting products requires time and effort. It is pleasant for parents and those accompanying them if, when visiting the pharmacy, their children can be entertained, for example with painting, in a well-supervised place.

CUSTOMER WC | These are still rare but very customer-friendly, offering customers the opportunity of using the toilet. Separate toilets for men and women are only necessary where demand is high.

NIGHT DISPENSARY | The nocturnal sale of medicines calls for facilities which makes this already complicated procedure easier for customers. The customer should be able to check which pharmacy is on night duty, ideally while protected from rain and cold, and announce his presence by means of a well-lit bell. Prescriptions and medicines are exchanged via a hatch in the immediate vicinity which should not be too large, in order to avoid robberies. The more of the customer the pharmacist can see, the greater his sense of safety. Increasingly, pharmacists are picking up on the American example of drive-in counters, which allow drivers to have direct contact with the pharmacy.

CONSULTING ROOM | The provision of a room which is both optically and acoustically insulated meets patients' need for privacy. It is above all senior citizens who value confidentiality when consulting the pharmacist. Ideally, this should be a closed room with seating and adequate space for movement, as this room should also be available for the provision of special services. During the fit-out, thought should be given to soundproofing measures; practical features here include an intercom to the dispensary, a video recorder, a PC, and a monitor, preferably with touchscreen.

INTENSIVE CONSULTING ROOM | Large pharmacies in particular face increased demand for consultancies, so that a second consultancy room is required. This fulfils the same functions as the room mentioned above, although ideally it should have a somewhat larger usable area for a comfortable seating group, so that conversations can be held with more than two people.

TREATMENT AND REST ROOM | In order to provide certain special services, larger pharmacies require a treatment and rest room which should be equipped with a divan. This room also serves as a reserve space for the future expansion of the consultancy and service range.

BEAUTY TREATMENT ROOM | In order to protect the privacy of customers having, say, facials, manicures or pedicures, a dedicated room is required which, however, as at a hairdresser's, may also contain two or more treatment stations.

ALPHABETICAL STORAGE | This term is now being widely used, although often reference is simply made to the pharmacy stockroom, the main feature of which is the alphabetical arrangement of the pharmaceutical preparations. Ideally, the storage cupboards, usually drawer racks, or racks of refrigerated cabinets, should be directly accessible from the dispensary. The alphabetical system may be dispensed with once a decision has been made to install an automated stockroom with a goods transport system.

WORK ROOM | Ideally located next to the stockroom, the work room is for the pharmacy assistants who manage the pharmacy stockroom, that means who keep it stocked and ensure that expiry dates are checked. The number of workplaces depends on the performance profile of the individual pharmacy.

PRESCRIPTION ROOM | According to the APBETRO, a compounding room is an essential room. It is used to directly manufacture certain delivery types of medicine, such as powders, creams, emulsions, tinctures, extracts, capsules, and mixtures. Special attention must be given here to the APBETRO, as well as to hygiene and Good Manufacturing Practices. As such, the prescription room must be in a protected area, separate from the customer area. This does not necessarily mean that it is not possible to see into this room, which recalls the pharmacy's roots in the apothecary's shop. For practical reasons, eye contact with the dispensary is also recommended.In fitting-out and equipping the prescription room, the APBETRO should be observed. Since industrially prepared delivery methods are increasingly pressing to the fore, prescription rooms are losing ground. However, individual pharmacies have recognised that there is potential to be activated here. Where space is limited, the prescription room can be combined with the laboratory. This jointly used room should have separated working areas and a minimum size of 15 square metres.

LAB | A well-performing laboratory requires Bunsen burners, heat sources, retorts, and annealing furnaces, and must also handle flammable liquids. It is therefore understandable that the construction and fit-out of a laboratory are governed by numerous regulations. The most important of these are the APBETRO, the building regulations of the given federal state, fire safety regulations and DIN 12924, Part 4[9]. These regulations govern, for example, the minimum area [12 square metres], the fire-resistant construction of walls, ceilings, and floors, a second escape route and, where work is undertaken with flammable liquids, an extractor with suction device, and at least one fire extinguisher. Attention should also be paid to good lighting, colourfast light, natural or mechanical ventilation, and surfaces which are easy to clean [Fig. 9].

WASHING ROOM | Where extensive and specialised lab work is undertaken, the installation of a washing room for cleaning containers and equipment actually is practical. Otherwise, as a standard feature, a washbasin and a special washing machine need to be built into the laboratory.

OFFICE | It is convenient to have a dedicated room for the undisturbed handling of office and administrative work which, despite computers, continues to increase. Under no circumstances should this room also serve as the night service room, as the personal feel is then lost. The office may also be used as a small in-house library for storing the scientific and other literature required under the APBETRO, such as the German Pharmacopoeia [Deutsche Arzneibuch], the European Pharmacopoeia, the German Drug Code, the Synonym List [Synonymverzeichnis], the Register of Standard Licensed Medical Products [Verzeichnis der Standardzulassungen], and the Provisions of the Applicable Pharmacy, Medicine, Narcotics, and Chemical laws [Fig. 10].

ARCHIVE | At least in larger pharmacies, a small archive for the orderly storage of files which inevitably accumulate over time is recommended, and this room can also be used for the storage of household items such as ladders or spare chairs [Fig. 11].

CYTOSTATICS ROOM | If cytostatics [substances which inhibit cell growth and cell partition] are prepared, a dedicated room is required.

For hygienic reasons, this room must contain a sluice for the personnel to change their clothes. In pharmacies which supply hospitals, depending on the medical performance profile, a room for parenteral nutrition [by subcutaneous injection] may be installed instead of or in addition to this room.

SERVICE ROOM – PHARMACIST | A personally organised service room generally meets the requirements of the manager of a larger pharmacy; this allows him to contribute to the pharmacy's performance. The room does not need to be large in size. Its well-designed interior represents the pharmacist's business philosophy.

NIGHT SERVICE ROOM | In accordance with the APBETRO, a night service room is one of the essential rooms which, if well designed, has the appearance of a comfortable hotel room. In the event that it is also used as a staff room – not prohibited but undesirable – instead of the preferable bed, a couch should be installed. The employee on night duty must have access to the pantry.

STAFF ROOM | § 29 of the German Workplace Directive [Arbeitsstättenverordnung[10]] states that if an establishment has more than ten employees, an easily accessible break room is required. In pharmacies, even where there are fewer employees, such a room should be installed, because the consumption of food at the workplace does not correspond with hygiene requirements. It is practical to arrange a pantry which, in larger pharmacies, can also take the shape of an individual room. A view of greenery outside is recommended as this enhances the employees' sense of relaxation.

STAFF CHANGING ROOMS | According to the German Workplace Directive, only one clothing storage unit and one locker for the storage of valuables are required per person. However, in the interests of both hygiene and the personnel themselves, small, individual changing rooms, divided by gender, are more suitable.

SANITARY ROOMS | The APBETRO requires that toilets for men and women, solely for the use of the staff, are required where an establishment has more than five employees. This means that a separate WC needs to be installed for customers. The installation of shower rooms depends on night service requirements. Shower rooms should contain a washbasin and may also be used by other employees. They should be beside the changing rooms and close to the night service room.

INCOMING GOODS ROOM | A dedicated room for incoming goods really is required because suppliers also deliver goods outside normal pharmacy opening hours, and these goods are initially deposited in this room. Packaging for example can

be removed here and preliminary sorting undertaken, and goods can also be prepared here for dispatch.

STOCKROOM | The size and type of stockroom has already been outlined in the "Data required for operation" chapter. In this description of the individual rooms, the type of goods being stocked is explored. According to Damaschke and Scheffer, there are considerable differences in the types of stock:

– proprietary medicinal products | In accordance with the APBETRO, the stockroom should contain at least one average week's supply of such products. There should be no negative impact on the quality of the medicines.
– vaccines | Defined temperatures subject to constant monitoring are prescribed.
– heat-sensitive medicines | Refrigerators or cooling units with three temperature levels are required.
– medicines which need to be stored very carefully | These are products which need to be kept under lock and key. Only specialised pharmaceutical personnel have access to them.
– highly toxic and toxic substances and toxic reagents | Here too, a lockable cabinet is required. The dispensing of these substances in regulated by the Chemicals Ban Ordinance.
– flammable liquids | the stockroom must be ventilated and should have no floor drain. Attention should be paid to escape routes.

– narcotics | The Narcotics Act requires that such products are separately stored and protected against unauthorised removal.
– medicines which require careful storage | The medicines in question are listed in the German Pharmacopoeia. Storage vessels must be marked in accordance with regulations.
– drugs | containers are to be protected against light and damp. Special advice on how to store individual drugs is provided in the German Pharmacopoeia.
– self-service products | Here it is merely necessary to ensure that these items are not mixed up with prescription-only products and medicines.

SPECIAL STOCKROOM | It should be decided from case to case as to which of the ten mentioned types of medicine should be stored in a special stockroom.

AUTOMATED STOCKROOM | The automated stockroom, outlined in the "Data required for operation" chapter, is meanwhile a feature of many pharmacies. Much positive feedback has been heard. Since several companies offer modular elements, such storage can be adapted well to given local conditions. When combined with automated transport systems, there is no need to place the automated stockroom in the immediate vicinity of the dispensary. This means that it is also possible to locate it on the floor below or above the pharmacy's main rooms. The space

thus gained in a functionally important place may be used for other purposes. The main advantage of the automated stockroom lies in the time saved by the pharmaceutical personnel, who no longer need to walk to and from the alphabetically-organised or other type of stockroom, and can therefore dedicate more time to advising customers. The use of new types of computer systems offers a further time saving to personnel: By improving ordering and supply capacity, stock is reduced and the administrative workload thus minimised [Fig. 12–13].

ORDER ROOM | In pharmacies which constantly supply a significant percentage of their goods to wholesale buyers such as group medical practices or hospitals, it is recommended that an order room be installed. This is where goods are assembled, where necessary packaged, and held ready for collection.

WASTE DISPOSAL ROOM | In order to avoid that waste is left lying around unsorted, pharmacies, including small pharmacies, should have a room with individual bins for the different types of waste, from which collection can be easily effected.

PLANT ROOM | Although highly desirable, owing to a lack of space or to a lack of coordination on the part of technical service providers, a dedicated room containing all technical connections, known as the plant room, is often not included in

Usable areas of a pharmacy
9 Laboratory
10 Office
11 Archive
12-13 Apotheke Zur Rose, Halle
    Logistics in a shipment pharmacy

draft plans. However, in terms of overview and servicing, such a room is most useful. In some of the presented projects it is regarded.

Key construction indicators

Alongside establishing qualitative features, some quantitative data is also important in evaluating a project.

Gross floor area | DIN 277 stipulates that the GFA is the sum of floor areas of all floor plan levels of a building in square metres. In relation to the usable areas which are specified above, this value gives an indication of the compactness of the building solution.

Gross room volume | DIN 277 stipulates that gross room area is the volume of the entire building contained within its outer boundary lines in cubic metres.

Construction costs | DIN 276 Building Construction Costs[11] serves as the basis for establishing construction costs. The cost groups 300 Building – Construction – and 400 Building – Technical Systems – are taken into consideration at this point.

In order to achieve comparability, costs should always contain the statutory rate of VAT. The cost of construction per cubic metre of gross room volume is often used as a comparison value.

Total costs | DIN 276 also applies here, with cost groups 200 to 700 being relevant. These are all costs including value added tax. The only exception are the costs of the plot, as these diverge widely depending on local conditions. The total costs are also known as investment costs. Taken together with the operating costs, they are important in deciding on a new pharmacy, expansion or redesign. A particularly important indicator here is total costs per square metre of usable area.

Parties involved in planning

With regard to construction in the healthcare sector, the formation of a committee to accompany the planning process has proven useful. Its objective is to examine all issues around planning and construction, and it attempts to find practical solutions which are ideally acceptable to all.

The main person in this group is the developer – this being either the pharmacist himself, or an outside investor. The job of coordination and direction is undertaken by a pharmacy planner. In general, this will be an independent architect or interior designer although, increasingly, it may also be a representative from a design company who specialises in the construction of pharmacies. Where the developer has no expertise of pharmacies, the pharmacist in charge of the pharmacy or responsible for operations management, ideally together with a

member of the pharmaceutical personnel, should be part of the planning team. Questions relating, in particular, to operational workflows, space allocation planning, and implementation planning are to be discussed in detail with these specialist individuals, who are involved in the pharmacy routine every day. The effort deployed here is worthwhile if constructional and organisational errors can thus be avoided.

Since the pharmacy's main brief is to provide services to customers, it can only be of advantage if their opinions are integrated into planning decisions. It is therefore a good idea to find an interested customer, who can accompany the planning process, offering criticism and suggestions. Alternatively or in addition, a customer survey can be carried out and the results integrated into planning. It can be useful to invite representatives of the licensing authorities to some of the planning committee's meetings.

PROJECT ELEMENTS

In general, pharmacies do not belong to the type of building designed by standard architects' offices. Rather, this is a specialised area for individual architects and interior designers who often have years of experience. Frequently, however, the work may be undertaken by an architect for whom the job represents a major challenge. The following remarks should primarily be of assistance to the architects, who are interested in

	Customer rooms	Business rooms	Special purpose rooms	Administrative rooms	Service and staff rooms	Supply and waste disposal	Training rooms	Plant rooms
Customer rooms		●	○	◔	○	○	●	◔
Business rooms	●		●	●	●	●	◔	●
Special purpose rooms	○	●		◔	●	●	◔	◔
Administrative rooms	◔	●	◔		●	◔	◔	◔
Service and staff rooms	○	●	●	●		◔	◔	◔
Supply and waste disposal	○	●	●	◔	◔		◔	●
Training rooms	●	◔	◔	◔	◔	◔		◔
Plant rooms	◔	●	◔	◔	◔	●	◔	

● Various functional relationships
● Certain functional relationships
● A few functional relationships
○ No functional relationships

14

designing pharmacies. They are also suitable for potential developers and operators, in providing an overview of the planning process.

Functions

Observation of functional workflows in pharmacies often make it possible to identify shortcomings and optimisation potential. As such, before building work starts, it is worthwhile undertaking a thorough examination of functional workflows and the resultant functional relationships, in order to ensure the smoothest and most effective operation. The following considers a few aspects of project planning.

FUNCTIONAL RELATIONSHIPS BETWEEN THE FUNCTIONAL GROUPS | One of the first areas to be considered for a project is the clarification of functional relationships between the functional groups. The strength of functional relationships is made clear in the corresponding matrix [Fig. 14]. There are three functional groups at the heart of the pharmacy: customer rooms, business rooms, and supply and waste disposal rooms. Depending on the size and performance profile of the pharmacy, the other functional groups cluster around this core needs to be taken into account.

FUNCTIONALLY PRACTICAL ARRANGEMENT OF THE FUNCTION GROUPS IN PHARMACIES WITH TWO OR THREE FLOORS | The matrix also allows conclusions to be drawn with regard to the arrangement of the functional groups in pharmacies with two or three floors. With several different levels, a greater effort is inevitably required for vertical paths. Whether these paths are via a well-located elevator, narrow, labyrinthine stairways or, possibly, even a tight spiral staircase is of major importance.

The schematic drawing [Fig. 15] shows the practical location of the functional groups for small, medium-sized, and large pharmacies arranged over two or three floors: The customer and business rooms are always immediately adjacent to one another. In multi-story pharmacies, the basement is a suitable location for the stockroom, whereby it is recommended that an elevator be installed, connecting the stockroom with the business rooms. Where the basement rooms have adequate daylight, social rooms can also be installed here, while service rooms are better located close to the business rooms. The upper floor may be used for the entire functional group of service and staff rooms.

INDIVIDUAL FUNCTIONS | On principle, the rooms belonging to the same functional group should ideally be close together – after all, this aspect was one reason why functional groups as such were created. There are also functional operations which call for close relationships between the individual functional groups. Thus the dispensary, which belongs to the functional

group "customer rooms", should have a very close relationship with the business rooms, in particular with the alphabetically-organised stockroom which, in some cases, even forms a single unit with the dispensary, separated from the customer area only by the sales counter. Furthermore, it should be easy to reach the stockroom from the incoming goods area, and there should be a short path from the stockroom to the "supply and waste disposal" functional group.

Some priorities should also be considered within the functional groups: The work room should be close to the alphabetically-organised stockroom. The prescription room and lab should ideally be located adjacent to one another or, as part of more affordable solutions, form a single unit.

FORMATION OF ZONES IN THE FLOOR PLAN | The pharmacy's floor plan is largely dependent on available floor space in a given building. Where the floor area can be chosen, or where a freestanding pharmacy building is being planned, consideration should be given to zoning the floor plan [Fig. 16]. The type of zoning determines the constructional nature of the pharmacy. Here, it is a question of arranging the pharmacy rooms from the viewpoint of the entering customers. A differentiation is made between pharmacies with one, two or three zones. The individual room zones may be immediately adjacent to one another or separated by hallways. In the case of a single zone

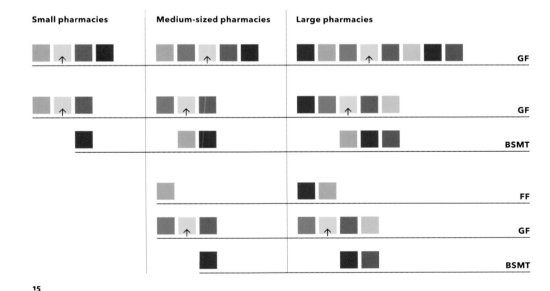

Small pharmacies	Medium-sized pharmacies	Large pharmacies	
			GF
			GF
			BSMT
			FF
			GF
			BSMT

15

14 Matrix of functional relationships between the functional groups

15 Arrangement of functional groups in one, two, and three-story buildings floor plan, all rooms are adjacent to each other; with two zones, the rooms are arranged behind one another while, with a three-zone floor plan, the rooms are staggered to an even greater depth. On principle, these arrangement variations apply in small, medium-sized, and large pharmacies in buildings with one, two or three floors, whereby three floors are not suitable for small pharmacies. The type of zoning and the number of floors are determining factors for the cost-effectiveness of a floor plan. It is generally held that because of the avoidance of vertical paths and the high degree of compactness, single story buildings with two or three zones offer the best solution in terms of building typology and energy consumption, irrespective of the size of the pharmacy. A measure of compactness is the circumference of the vertical outer surfaces [U]. This value is by far the lowest for the two recommended solutions.

Daylight

In recent decades, demand for rooms with daylight has risen considerably. On principle, it is considered that staff rooms and rooms in which work is performed for longer periods should receive daylight. There are different regulations with regard to the length of time in the various federal states. Solutions which provide daylight in as many work and staff rooms as possible are seen as the way forward. Bearing in mind the remarks about daylight mentioned in the "space

allocation plan" section, the architects face the challenge of finding means, including technical ones, which provide the pharmacy's employees with daylight.

Orientation

That people and, in this case, senior citizens in particular have problems with orientation is surely connected with information overload. The entrance itself is very often a psychological threshold. Walking through the pharmacy past vast numbers of shelves packed with goods, can feel like wandering in a maze. Lighting and colour markings on ceilings and walls can be useful here, as can the choice of flooring to mark specific routes, the avoidance of excessive product choice and, especially, the clear and well-organised positioning of the built-in and mobile furniture.

Technical fit-out

The sources of requirements governing the technical fit-out were discussed above in "Legislation, ordinances, and other regulations". Because of their wide scope, only a brief outline of explanations with regard to technical fit-out can be provided here.

STATICS | In the case of refurbishment, the planner must work with the existing static conditions, largely for economic reasons. In the case of new constructions, however, he should use

the statics in order to achieve as broad a span width as possible. This creates wide spaces which are not divided or interrupted by walls or supports, allowing greater scope for design and flexibility for changes.

VENTILATION | The pharmacy should convey as many impressions on the senses as possible, proffering the scent of medicines is a questionable undertaking, as individual sensitivities vary greatly. The installation of an easily-controllable, effective ventilation system is required to provide a neutral level of ventilation. Perhaps, after further experiments, scents with a health-promoting effect may be dispersed through ventilation systems.

HEATING, COOLING, AIR HUMIDITY, AND FILTERING | The German Workplace Directive requires a minimum temperature of 21° C and a maximum temperature of 25° C in work rooms. This also provides a comfortable temperature for customers. Comfort also means that on hot days, a soothing coolness and pleasant air humidity are provided, since dry air has a negative effect on the airways. With regard to allergy sufferers, filtering the incoming air is good. Conventional heating systems, cooling equipment, humidifiers, and filters can take care of these needs.

AIR CONDITIONING | The requirements mentioned above can all be resolved by a modern air conditioning system. In new constructions, the

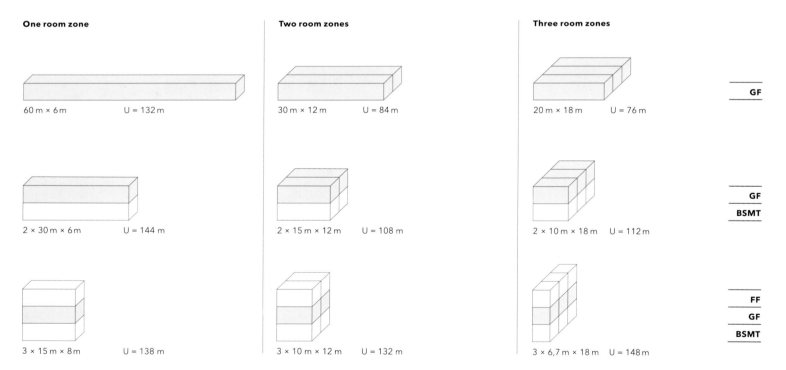

One room zone

60 m × 6 m　　　U = 132 m

2 × 30 m × 6 m　　U = 144 m

3 × 15 m × 8 m　　U = 138 m

Two room zones

30 m × 12 m　　　U = 84 m

2 × 15 m × 12 m　　U = 108 m

3 × 10 m × 12 m　　U = 132 m

Three room zones

20 m × 18 m　　　U = 76 m　　　GF

2 × 10 m × 18 m　　U = 112 m　　GF
BSMT

3 × 6,7 m × 18 m　　U = 148 m　　FF
GF
BSMT

decision to install such equipment must be made before planning starts. Retrofitting is a major undertaking. A properly adjusted air conditioning system offers the advantage of controllable climate without draughts and irritating noise. Space is also saved as no heaters are required. It should be checked in good time whether the investment and operating costs can be kept within reasonable bounds, and an estimate made of how much this air – which might be the healthiest around – is worth.

ACOUSTICS | Reducing noise pollution is one of the main tasks of environmental protection today. The building regulations of the federal states already call for protection against the transmission of airborne sound within buildings. DIN 4109[12] contains requirements with regard to rooms and construction elements; the German Workplace Directive regulates noise levels in work and staff rooms. These requirements may be fulfilled by separating construction elements through the right choice of floors to reduce impact sound and airborne sound, the use of acoustic ceilings and sound-absorbent wall coverings, the type of fit-out and furnishing, and the use of sound-absorbing doors.

LIGHTING | Exterior and internal lighting requirements are discussed in "Design elements" above. The planning of lighting systems is a highly complex and interrelated issue and should therefore, in the interests of the pharmacy's overall appearance, be carried out by a qualified specialist.

BURGLARY PROTECTION | It is not merely the monetary value of the medicines, but also the attraction exercised by certain drugs which give rise to an increased risk of burglary. This cannot be prevented altogether but may at least be reduced with the large-scale use of technology. Fittings in this area are usually metal shutters and pull-down grilles as well as high-resistance safety glass and motion detectors with lights and sonic alarms. Video surveillance systems, in this case, have also proven useful, as these can help to identify burglars. A radio connection to the nearest police station finally can lead to an early arrest.

FIRE PROTECTION | Great attention is dedicated to the prevention of fire in pharmacies, particularly in labs. The building regulations of the federal states, the German Workplace Directive, DIN 4102[13], the Health and Safety Authorities [Amt für Arbeitsschutz] and the Professional Accident Prevention and Insurance Associations [Berufsgenossenschaften] devote considerable attention to the prevention of fire in pharmacies, particularly in laboratory rooms. There are requirements with regard to the fire-resistance class of supporting and non-supporting construction elements, and the fire behaviour of the building materials. The length and number of escape routes are also defined. Pharmacies must have a minimum of three fire extinguishers. In particularly dangerous areas, the installation of fire alarms and sprinkler systems is recommended.

Special features of refurbishment
In general, refurbishments are carried out to repair wear and tear in the fit-out and building substance. In addition, it is usually hoped to better exploit the area and space and to optimise workflows. In recent times, it is changes to the technical fit-out, such as the installation of a new lighting system, heating, ventilation, cooling or filtering systems, or the installation of complete air conditioning systems or, in conjunction with the establishment of an automated stockroom, the creation of a transport system, which are common reasons for minor or major construction work.

While the construction of a new construction is subject only to the requirement to be completed by a given deadline, refurbishments, including expansions and redesigns, are associated with considerably greater difficulties. The temporary closure of the business premises usually ensures the fastest completion of the work but, for economic reasons, this solution is usually not chosen, so that construction work has to take place alongside normal business. Dustproof sheeting is required to protect customers and personnel and to preserve hygiene. Such sheets should also contribute to reducing the noise of the building work.

16 Diagrams of one, two, and three-story pharmacies with one to three room zones. For reasons of clarity, the verticals are shown in superelevation. The enclosed space is the same size in all diagrams. "U" represents the circumference of the outer surfaces in metres.

PT	FUNCTIONAL GROUP FUNCTIONAL UNIT FUNCTIONAL ELEMENT	ILLUMINATION	USABLE AREA IN SQM	
1	**Customer rooms**			**56**
1.1	Sales area with self-service area, behind- the-counter shelves, cash-desk, and night dispensing area	○	50	
1.2	Consultations	○	6	
2	**Business rooms**			**46**
2.1	Laboratory	○	12	
2.2	Prescription area	○	6	
2.3	Workstation [and office]	○	12	
2.4	Alphabetic storage	○	16	
3	**Service and staff rooms**			**32**
3.1	Night shift room	○	10	
3.2	Staff lounge and kitchen	○	8	
3.3	Staff changing | Women			
3.3.1	Staff changing	◉	4	
3.3.2	Shower	●	2	
3.4	Staff changing | Men			
3.4.1	Staff changing	◉	2	
3.4.2	Shower	●	2	
3.5	Bathroom – Staff | Women			
3.5.1	Vestibule	●	1	
3.5.2	Bathroom	●	1	
3.6	Bathroom – Staff | Men			
3.6.1	Vestibule	●	1	
3.6.2	Bathroom	●	1	
4	**Supply and waste disposal**			**26**
4.1	Goods inwards	◉	4	
4.2	Product storage	●	16	
4.3	Cleaning equipment storage and disposal room	●	6	

Usable area of a small pharmacy **160**

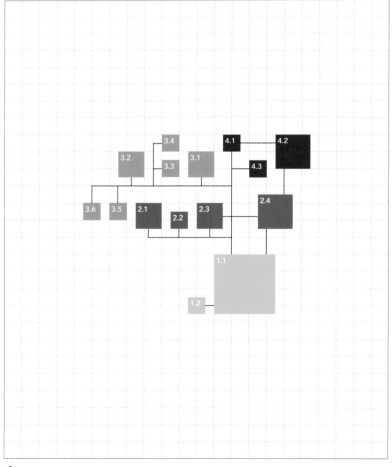

17

18

It is usually necessary to relocate certain facilities or specialist rooms. In such cases, careful thought should be given to how the business can continue to operate during the individual building phases without too much additional effort. Refurbishments involve unpleasantness for all parties concerned. It is therefore advisable to apologise for any inconvenience in advance.

STANDARD SPACE ALLOCATION PLANS, FUNCTIONAL DIAGRAMS, AND STANDARD FLOOR PLANS

The space allocation plans, functional diagrams, and floor plans shown here for small, medium-sized, and large pharmacies serve to explain the principles of operation and construction in one standard example each. Standard in this instance means a sample or model for the minimum effort required to achieve a functional and cost-effective solution.

For the space allocation plans, the explanation provided in "Breakdown into functional groups" above is used. The space allocation plans also contain a comment on lighting [see "Space allocation plans" above]. A differentiation is made between individual rooms [functional elements] and rooms which belong directly together [functional units]. The suffix plan ID numbers designate the functional group and, consecutively in each case, the functional units and functional elements.

The functional diagrams show all rooms and their functional relationships. The different squares used as symbols for the rooms should give a rough indication of the size of the given usable area.

The standard floor plans are not intended to be a model for plans. In the deliberately chosen single-story form shown here, they merely represent a visualisation of the space allocation plans and are thus confirmation of the latter's feasibility and an aid to orientation when commencing planning. Plans are the sole remit of architects, interior designers, and other pharmacy planners who, using their creativity and design skills, work together with pharmacists and their employees to come up with individual solutions.

Standards for a small pharmacy
For small pharmacies with a usable area of up to 175 square metres, it is particularly important to comply with the provisions of the APBETRO with regard to minimum size. These state that a pharmacy must consist of a dispensary, a laboratory, a storage, and a night service room. These rooms must have a usable area of at least 110 square metres. These provisions do not make reference to the necessary service and staff rooms.

SPACE ALLOCATION PLAN AND FUNCTIONAL DIAGRAM FOR A SMALL PHARMACY | The minimum size required by the APBETRO is met by the following

space allocation plan [Fig. 17], which has an area of 116 square metres [dispensary with consulting room 56 square metres, laboratory 12 square metres, prescription room 6 square metres, alphabetical storage and stockroom 32 square metres, and night service room 10 square metres]. Together with necessary expansions, this gives a usable area of 160 square metres, a value which should not be undercut. In selecting this size, it should be ensured that expansion is possible through the construction of an annexe, or by using rooms on a lower or upper floor in order to take future developments into account. The functional relationships between the rooms in the space allocation plan are relatively simply and easily implemented [Fig. 18].

Because of the economical layout of the space allocation plan, dedicated rooms are not available for some functions. Thus, for example, there are no dedicated areas for special purposes [children's play area, washing room, special lab, archive, pharmacist's service room, special stockroom, and waste disposal room]. Furthermore, the "training" functional area is absent. If space-saving automatic systems are used, usage of the areas for alphabetical storage and the medical stockroom can be optimised.

FLOOR PLAN FOR A SMALL PHARMACY | The schematic floor plan [Fig. 19, 20] is broken down into three zones with slight overlaps: the customer zone, the business room zone, and the storage and staff

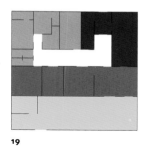

19

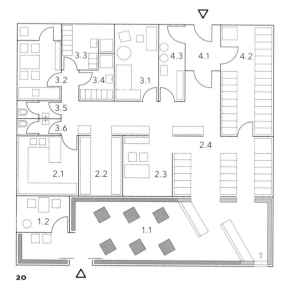

20

17 Sample space allocation plan for a small pharmacy
18 Functional diagram of a small pharmacy
19 Diagrammatic plan of the floor plan
To scale 1:400
20 Standard floor plan for a small pharmacy
Dark grey: self-service range
Light grey: over-the-counter products
To scale 1:200

PT	FUNCTIONAL GROUP FUNCTIONAL UNIT FUNCTIONAL ELEMENT	ILLUMINATION	USABLE AREA IN SQM
1	**Customer rooms**		**124**
1.1	Sales area with self-service area, behind-the-counter shelves, and cash-desk	○	74
1.2	Special purpose rooms		
1.2.1	Beauty treatment	○	8
1.2.2	Spa treatment	○	8
1.2.3	Other areas	○	10
1.3	Night service dispensary	●	2
1.4	Consulting	○	8
1.5	Treatment and rest room	○	12
1.6	Bathroom – Customers | Unisex		
1.6.1	Vestibule	●	1
1.6.2	Bathroom	●	1
2	**Business rooms**		**66**
2.1	Laboratory	○	14
2.2	Prescription area	○	10
2.3	Workstation	○	10
2.4	Washing room	◐	8
2.5	Alphabetic storage	○	24
3	**Administrative rooms**		**20**
3.1	Office	○	14
3.2	Archive	●	6
4	**Service and staff rooms**		**54**
4.1	Service room – Pharmacist	○	8
4.2	Night shift room	○	12
4.3	Staff lounge and kitchen	○	16
4.4	Staff changing | Women		
4.4.1	Staff changing	◐	6
4.4.2	Shower	●	2
4.5	Staff changing | Men		
4.5.1	Staff changing	◐	4
4.5.2	Shower	●	2
4.6	Bathroom – Staff | Women		
4.6.1	Vestibule	●	1
4.6.2	Bathroom	●	1
4.7	Bathroom – Staff | Men		
4.7.1	Vestibule	●	1
4.7.2	Bathroom	●	1
5	**Supply and waste disposal**		**56**
5.1	Goods inwards	◐	8
5.2	Storage		
5.2.1	Product storage	●	30
5.2.2	Drug storage	●	8
5.3	Cleaning equipment storage	●	6
5.4	Waste disposal room	●	4
Usable area of a medium-sized pharmacy			**320**

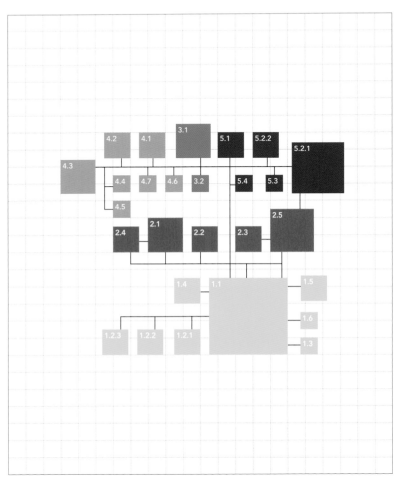

room zone. Incoming goods are transferred to the medical stockroom or to alphabetical storage, which has a direct link with the medical stockroom. The dispensary, which is parallel to the façade, has plenty of daylight and a curved customer path which leads to the two sales counters via numerous products displayed on wall shelving and in mobile containers. The dispensing counter for night service is conveniently located for the pharmacy personnel. All rooms in the central zone can be supplied with daylight if generous glazing is used.

Standards for a medium-sized pharmacy

This category's upper size limit of 320 square metres of usable area, as a basic principle, allows for a well-equipped pharmacy.

SPACE ALLOCATION PLAN AND FUNCTIONAL DIAGRAM FOR A MEDIUM-SIZED PHARMACY | With the exception of the special purpose rooms and the rooms for training, all functional groups are in evidence. The special purpose room also provides space for expanding the product range, while the treatment and rest room can also be used for healthcare services [Fig. 21, 22]. The pharmacist has his own service room, and there is a special stockroom.

FLOOR PLAN FOR A MEDIUM-SIZED PHARMACY | Because of the short paths involved, a roughly square floor plan divided into three zones has

been chosen [Fig. 23, 24]: the customer zone, the business zone, the zone for the administrative, service and staff rooms, and the supply and waste disposal rooms. Where generous glazing is used in the rooms adjacent to the customer area, all rooms in which the staff spend longer periods of time have daylight. Practical transport is installed from the incoming goods area to the stockroom, and from there to alphabetical storage. The business rooms are conveniently located adjacent to each other; the same goes for the service and staff rooms. From the office, incoming goods can be directly monitored. The dispensary, also arranged lengthwise here, makes it possible for passers-by to get a glimpse in through the shelves. There is also plenty of light in the room above the shelves. The customers reach the three sales counters after they have had the chance to look at the self-service range. Other products are displayed on the shelves and in the hanging elements of the over-the-counter section. In a medium-sized pharmacy, the dispensary should also have a consultancy room, a treatment and rest room, a waiting area, and a WC. Customers have access to the night dispensary immediately beside the slightly recessed entrance.

Standards for a large pharmacy

SPACE ALLOCATION PLAN AND FUNCTIONAL DIAGRAM FOR A LARGE PHARMACY | All functional groups are represented here [Fig. 25, 26]. In even larger

pharmacies, for example those in hospitals, there are, in particular, several special purpose rooms and other usable areas for training. Using an area of 480 square metres, the space allocation plan represents the average size for large pharmacies.

Floor plan for a large pharmacy | A shape resembling a square is also chosen for the floor plan of a large pharmacy, as this shortens paths [Fig. 27, 28]. Here too, three zones are foreseen which, because of the chosen floor plan shape, give rise to partial overlaps. Despite the necessary staggered depth of the floor plan, almost all rooms in which employees spend longer periods have daylight, whereby it is required that the walls oriented towards the customer area have generous expanses of glass. In the case of the centrally located order room, above the alphabetical storage and connected with the stockroom, a skylight can help to provide those working there with a glimpse of the sky. The pharmacist's room, located beside the office with integrated library, offers a good overview of incoming and outgoing goods. The staff rooms form an interconnected unit. Customers are offered rooms for discreet and intensive consultation, a treatment and rest room with waiting room, a lecture and seminar room with cloakroom, a children's play corner which they can see clearly, and toilets for men and women, all directly accessible from the dispensary. In large pharmacies too, the customer's path leads him to the sales counters at the rear of the room via a range

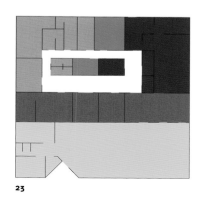

23

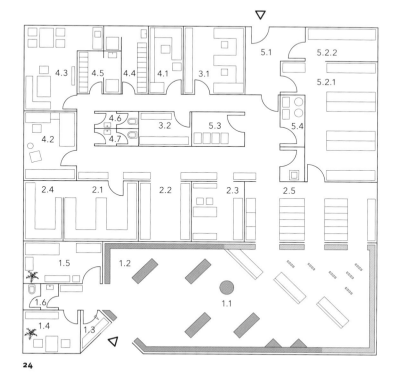

24

21 Sample space allocation plan for a medium-sized pharmacy
22 Functional diagram of a medium-sized pharmacy
23 Diagrammatic plan of the floor plan
  To scale 1:400
24 Standard floor plan for a medium-sized pharmacy
  Dark grey: self-service range
  Light grey: over-the-counter products
  To scale 1:200

PT	FUNCTIONAL GROUP FUNCTIONAL UNIT FUNCTIONAL ELEMENT	ILLUMINATION	USABLE AREA IN SQM
1	**Customer rooms**		**176**
1.1	Sales area with self-service area, behind-the-counter shelves, and cash-desk	○	90
1.2	Special purpose rooms		
1.2.1	Beauty treatment	○	12
1.2.2	Spa treatment	○	12
1.2.3	Other areas	○	14
1.3	Children's play area	○	6
1.4	Night service dispensary	●	4
1.5	Consulting	○	6
1.6	Intensive consulting	○	10
1.7	Treatment		
1.7.1	Waiting room	◐	6
1.7.2	Treatment and rest room	○	12
1.8	Bathroom – Customers | Women		
1.8.1	Vestibule	●	1
1.8.2	Bathroom	●	1
1.9	Bathroom – Customers | Men		
1.9.1	Vestibule	●	1
1.9.2	Bathroom	●	1
2	**Business rooms**		**82**
2.1	Laboratory	○	16
2.2	Prescription area	○	12
2.3	Workstation	○	10
2.4	Washing room	◐	8
2.5	Alphabetic storage	○	36
3	**Special purpose rooms**		**10**
3.1	Special lab	○	10
4	**Administrative rooms**		**26**
4.1	Office	○	18
4.2	Archive	○	8
5	**Service and staff rooms**		**68**
5.1	Service room – Pharmacist	○	10
5.2	Night shift room	○	12
5.3	Staff rest area		
5.3.1	Staff lounge	○	18
5.3.2	Kitchen	○	4
5.4	Staff changing | Women		
5.4.1	Staff changing	◐	8
5.4.2	Shower	●	4
5.5	Staff changing | Men		
5.5.1	Staff changing	◐	6
5.5.2	Shower	●	2
5.6	Bathroom – Staff | Women		
5.6.1	Vestibule	●	1
5.6.2	Bathroom	●	1
5.7	Bathroom – Staff | Men		
5.7.1	Vestibule	●	1
5.7.2	Bathroom	●	1
6	**Supply and waste disposal**		**88**
6.1	Goods inwards	◐	10
6.2	Storage		
6.2.1	Product storage	●	36
6.2.2	Drug storage	●	14
6.2.3	Packaging material and window dressing	●	4
6.3	Order picker	○	12
6.4	Cleaning equipment storage	●	6
6.5	Waste disposal room	●	4
7	**Training rooms**		**30**
7.1	Training		
7.1.1	Cloakroom	◐	4
7.1.2	Lecture and seminar room	●	26
	Usable area of a large pharmacy		**480**

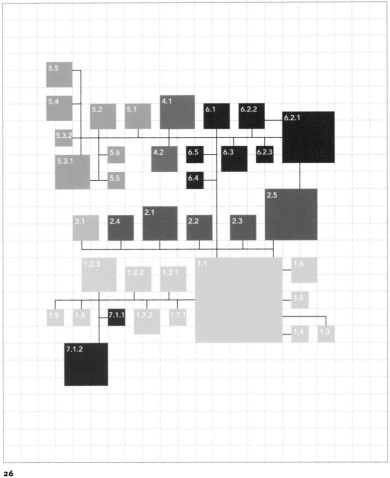

of shelves and mobile containers displaying additional product offers. Customers requiring night service can avail of a small room, accessible from outside the pharmacy, which is also practical during harsh winter weather.

DESIGN ELEMENTS

Exterior architecture

The appearance of some buildings reveals their purpose. In terms of the importance that pharmacies can have in daily life, this kind of identification would be most helpful. Designers should feel compelled to find suitable architectural means to create an unmistakable image for pharmacies.

BUILDING STRUCTURE | Pharmacies usually occupy parts of several-story buildings, which may be residential or commercial properties, department stores, shopping centres, group medical practices, railway stations or airports. In such cases, the pharmacy is normally required to fit in with the existing exterior architecture. However, some pharmacies are also designed as individual buildings, and it is here that a distinctive pharmacy design is possible. The shaping of such buildings – mainly in a range from one story to three storys at most – can be used to make them attractive to customers and to suggest the appeal of a visit. In general, imagination and shape vocabulary have no boundaries.

However, despite the desirable differentiation, it is recommended that the pharmacy architecture take the landscape and the surrounding buildings into consideration. As Mies van der Rohe famously exhorted – less is more.

FAÇADE | In terms of the façade too, very different looks are possible, depending on whether the pharmacy is part of a greater structure or an individual building. In the first instance, there is often only the possibility of affixing illuminated elements with the pharmacy "green cross" symbol ["A" in Germany] and the name of the pharmacy. In the second case, there is considerably more scope for design, using open and closed walls, expressive materials, a diverse range of colours, and by playing with light and shadow. Here too, information overload should be avoided, as this does not fit in with the essentially serious nature of the pharmacy.

ENTRANCE | For customers, who are often not in the best of health, the main entrance to the pharmacy should be clearly identifiable from a considerable distance, including for people who are unfamiliar with the area or those with disabilities. It is often wise to create one or more side entrances, in order to shorten customer paths. It is also helpful to design an entrance which acts as a magnet, and to install nocturnal illumination. Automatic doors and barrier freedom ease access for customers with

wheelchairs and pushchairs/prams. The APBETRO requires that the opening hours and the rota service list be displayed at the entrance. The Trade, Commerce, and Industry Regulation Act specifies that the proprietor's name must also be shown directly there.

SHOP WINDOWS | In shop design terms, the primary function of shop windows is to display the goods on offer inside. While old pharmacies often only had windows for illumination, newer pharmacies are usually fitted with large display windows, which advertise new products more or less aggressively.

Unfortunately, this often blocks the view of the usually interesting interior of the pharmacy. As such, many pharmacists today dispense with the presentation of products in the shop windows, and use the generous window space to create a sense of transparency and openness, in order to generate trust. In arranging shelving on glazed outer walls, clever design should ensure that the interior is still visible, thus arousing curiosity and the desire to enter the pharmacy.

EXTERIOR LIGHTING | The exterior lighting should attract customers, ease orientation, and it should as well create the right mood. Special attention should always be paid to the pharmacys' entrance. The strength of the illumination should be adjusted to the level of lighting in the surrounding area, in order to avoid glare.

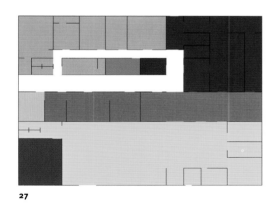

27

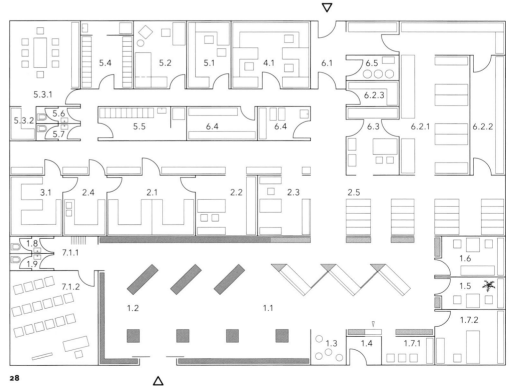

28

25 Sample space allocation plan for a large pharmacy
26 Functional diagram of a large pharmacy
27 Diagrammatic plan of the floor plan
To scale 1:400
28 Standard floor plan for a large pharmacy
Dark grey: self-service range
Light grey: over-the-counter products
To scale 1:200

Interior design

The planner has a broad palette of architectural design of interior spaces in pharmacies from which to choose. Armed with his creative experience, a well developed sense of quality, and a knowledge of the effects of hard and soft shapes, harsh and soft colours, light and shadow, and the use of materials, he should approach his work with a loving eye to detail.

BUILT-IN AND FREESTANDING FURNITURE | One of the primary goals of the pharmacy planner should be to create an individual feel, and this can be best achieved with built-in furniture. The exclusive use of mass-produced furniture is less suitable for this purpose; however, the cost of custom-made designer furniture is often incompatible with the available budget, so the planner needs to find a carefully balanced solution. All of the furnishing elements should form an overarching design concept, which expresses the desired image of the pharmacy. In order to preserve customer privacy, the once usually large single point of sale [POS] is now commonly replaced by several individual POS, which should be kept clear of goods. Such units should ideally include an integrated till, an integrated coin tray, and the necessary computer equipment [monitor, keyboard, price display, scanner, and photocopier]. Other small but important details include bag hooks or holders for customers' mobility aids, so that they can carry on a conversation with the pharmacist and inform themselves on the product range without distractions, as well as floor markings which designate the desirable distance to be kept from the customer being served.

The alphabetical storage area with drawer cabinets for storing medicines, often in modular form offering a high degree of flexibility, is close by. Two alphabetical storage units might also be considered: A unit for products which are turned over quickly, close to the sales tables, and an additional unit for other products which may be installed further to the rear. Alternatively, medicines can be stored in an automated warehouse and transported to the individual POS by pressing a button.

Before reaching the POS, the customer has a chance to select his own self-service products. For practical reasons, these are located in individual mobile shelf units or display gondolas, organised by product type. Shelves containing over-the-counter products are arranged behind the POS. Where the size of the pharmacy permits, furnishings should also include a seating group and a children's play area.

INTERIOR LIGHTING | In a somewhat adapted form, the same principles applying to exterior lighting go for interior spaces. Light accompanies the customer from the moment of entry and makes orientation easier. Accent lighting points the way to specific products in the self-service and over-the-counter displays. In selecting lighting, attention should be paid to correct colour reproduction and a comfortable atmosphere which may be achieved using a warm white light. In some places, thought should be given to where the light falls, to avoid the irritating formation of shadows. Work rooms should be adequately lit, without glare or monitor reflections, aiming for low energy consumption and low heat load. The minimum requirements of DIN 5035[14] and the provisions of the German Workplace Directive must be met.

SURFACES | Visible at all times and usually also tactile, the surfaces of fittings, furniture, equipment, walls, ceilings, and floors represent the main objects of design work and challenges. For each object, the planner has to select materials from an almost unlimited range of possibilities, and decide on a certain surface structure and colour.

For fittings and furniture, natural surfaces with their integral colours and man-made surfaces with a large choice of colours are available. The choice, made in keeping with the overall concept, should also give thought to resilience and easiness to clean. For hygienic reasons, equipment should be made of durable materials which are not subject to wear and tear. With regard to walls, differentiations should be made: In general, plaster which can be painted in white or colour, or papered over, is adequate; for operational and sanitary rooms, washable wall coverings should be used. Ceilings are usually suspended to make room for

lighting, transport systems, ventilation, and air conditioning. Because of the easy accessibility required for servicing, they are usually made of cassettes which are often also used for improving the acoustics. To date, only a few examples of ceilings being used as a playground for imaginative design have been discovered. When choosing the right flooring, a range of aspects needs to be considered: The intended effect of the flooring in the overall design concept, the existing fitting dimensions, particularly in light of future redesigns, resilience, sound absorption, skid resistance, easiness of cleaning, and, crucially, cost-effectiveness. In laying flooring at the entrance area, one should not forget to build in a sufficiently large, floor flush doormat.

With all surface objects, colours have a major impact on the overall appearance, and thus also have a psychological effect on customers and personnel. According to Frieling, colours may be calming, aggressive, oppressive, encouraging, alienating, soft, alarming, stimulating, warming, eyecatching, constricting, securing, comforting, confusing, distracting, cold, alerting, heightening, cooling, intensifying, glowing, communicative, activating, light, covering, fostering, and relaxing[15]. Well-dosed colour can therefore promote orientation in a given space, alter proportions, and furthermore stimulate certain moods. Too many different colours should be avoided as this usually only achieves a short-term effect.

ELEMENTS OF PLANNING AND CONSTRUCTION PROCESS

Identification of basic data

Once the idea of expanding, converting or refurbishing an existing pharmacy, or of erecting a new construction has been sparked, the developer, together with other stakeholders, must compile a list of basic data, the most important of which are outlined below. These comments are only discussed briefly, as these are jobs which must anyway be performed by experienced and qualified specialist planners.

LOCATION ANALYSIS | In planning a new pharmacy, the choice of location for the future business should not be left to chance. Rather, before any further decisions are made, a thorough analysis of the relevant facts should be made. Distances from existing, competing pharmacies [pharmacy density] are important, as are proximity to medical practices, group medical practices or other medical facilities, the transport situation, location in relation to means of transport, population density, projected level of casual customers, size and purchasing power of potential target groups [families, singles, senior citizens], and plot prices.

The necessary assessment and weighting of the numerous different aspects in the event of alternative locations, and the recommendation of a preferred solution, call for a great deal of experience and should be placed in the hands of a specialist, who can help to ensure that such expenditure is worthwhile.

MASTER PLANNING | Because of numerous flawed decisions with regard to construction measures, experts have for some years been advocating master planning. This works out the basics for operation and construction [and may also include the location analysis mentioned above]. In the case of redesigns, a target/actual comparison is carried out, schematic variants for reaching targets developed, and, finally, a proposal made for the chosen solution on the basis of the analysis, and with due consideration for projected investment and operating costs. Master planning should also include the pharmacy's potential future development and plan in corresponding scope for possible alterations and expansions. Supplementary sheet 4 of DIN 13080 "Division of Hospitals into Functional Areas and Functional Sections – Masterplanning for General Hospitals" contains comments which also apply to pharmacies.

TIME PLANNING | Alongside the estimated timing of the planning process as projected in the master plan, where a specific construction measure has been decided, precise time planning forms a major element of planning. Precise periods and completion deadlines are drawn up for all phases. An element of effective time planning is ongoing monitoring and, where required, updating. Based

Paracelsus-Apotheke, Lünen
29 Coulors are a dominant feature of the appearance of the pharmacy.
(Architect: Renate Hawig)
Hubertus-Apotheke, Dorsten-Wulfen
30 If coulors, materials, and structures are inherently consistent, a harmonious atmosphere will be created.
(Architect: Renate Hawig)

on the motto "time is money", punctual completion of construction can avoid the considerable extra costs which are inevitably associated with overrun deadlines. This applies in particular to refurbishments and redesigns which are carried out while the business continues its daily operations. The disturbance and unpleasantness usually suffered by customers and personnel in such situations should not continue for even a single day longer than is absolutely necessary.

SPACE ALLOCATION PLANNING | Once the basics of the pharmacy project have been established, a space allocation plan has to be drawn up. Here too, specialised planners should ideally be used, who must undertake this assignment together with the pharmacy manager and his staff right from the outset. Details of the formal breakdown and necessary details are shown in the earlier chapter "Data required for construction". It should be ensured that the space allocation plan shows each room with its required usable area. Rough sketches for critical rooms should already be prepared, which will provide an explanation of the specified usable area values. A good space allocation plan will not omit any rooms [including the caretaker's room]; developing rooms will be given a suitable reserve of space, and no unnecessary space will be demanded, as not only will its construction call for major expenditure, but it must also be operated above and beyond the pharmacy's lifetime.

COST PLANNING | The developer must consider the investment costs arising out of construction measures at all times, but particularly when commencing planning. The developer wishes to get an overview of costs at as early a stage as possible, so that he can feel secure in making fundamental decisions. If he knows the cost framework, for example, he has the opportunity to select the appropriate design option and standard of fit-out.

With regard to new constructions or expansions, there are processes which allow a rough estimation of costs immediately after the space allocation plan has been drawn up. According to the cost category process developed by the *Institut für Wirtschaftliches Bauen* in Bremen, an established cost can be allocated to the usable areas of the individual types of room on the basis of analyses conducted throughout Germany. In this way, a total cost can then be calculated. A rougher estimate of the projected costs can also be obtained using pharmacy-specific empirically established costs per square metre of usable area. This value needs to be modified accordingly in keeping with different local and chronological factors and, of course, for differing standards.

For redesigns and refurbishments, the above methods can only be used to a limited extent because of the wide range of variations. It is first and foremost the longstanding experience of qualified planners which is required.

Planning fees

Clause 15 of the Fee Structure for Architects and Engineers [HOAI][16] specifies the fees to be paid by the client. A differentiation is made between new constructions, new plant, reconstruction, expansion, redesign, modernisation, spatial expansion, maintenance, and restoration. Based on services, the fees are broken down into nine different fee groups; important ones are briefly outlined below.

PRE-PLANNING | The most important basic services are the analysis of the basic data, the drafting of a planning concept, including the examination of alternative options, the clarification and explanation of relevant urban construction, design, functional, technical, physical construction, economic and energy-related aspects, pre-negotiations with authorities, and an estimate of costs in line with DIN 276. Special services include, for example, the creation of a financing plan, or a building and operational cost-benefit analysis.

DRAFT PLANNING | Basic services largely comprise the drawing of a plan on a scale of 1:100 and, for spatial expansions on a scale of 1:50 and 1:20, negotiations with authorities and other specialists involved in planning with regard to approvability and an estimate of costs in line with DIN 276.

IMPLEMENTATION PLANNING | This phase involves the final implementation, detail and construction drawings on a scale of 1:50 to 1:1, including

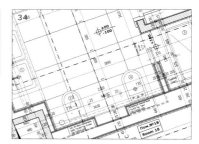

determination of the materials. For pharmacies, in general these plans are particularly important because they fundamentally fix the design of the details.

PROJECT MONITORING | Once the "Preparation" and "Collaboration in awarding the contract" basic services [which we have skipped here] have been provided, project monitoring has the aim of overseeing the completion of the job in keeping with the building permit and all mandatory requirements with regard to individual aspects of the design.

The basic services in this phase also include the creation of a time schedule, an estimate of costs in line with DIN 276, an application for final certification from the authorities, and de-snagging. This basic service comprises 31 percent – almost one-third – of the total fees.

COMMISSIONING PLAN | Although this does not form part of the HOAI services, a detailed commissioning plan can be very practical. Particularly for building work carried out during normal business operations, a gradual, ideally interruption-free transition from the outset is desirable. An inauguration party with interesting lectures, drinks, small gifts, and special offers can be very useful in winning customer loyalty and for advertising purposes. The author of this work, anyway, very much looks forward to receiving such invitations.

Planning and construction process
31 Signing of a contract
32 Conception sketches
33 Building licence
34 Construction documentation
35 Production of furniture
36 Building site inspection
37 Documentary report

SOURCES

1 Bundesvereinigung Deutscher Apothekerverbände: Die Apotheke. Zahlen, Daten, Fakten. Berlin 2007.

2 Apothekenbetriebsordnung of 26 September 1995. Bundesgesetzblatt I. Page 1195 and Page 1574

3 Gesetz über das Apothekenwesen [Apothekengesetz–ApoG] of 15 Oktober 1980, Bundesgesetzblatt I. Page 874

4 Robert-Koch-Institut: Anforderungen der Hygiene an die funktionelle und bauliche Gestaltung und den Betrieb von krankenhauseigenen und das Krankenhaus versorgenden Apotheken. Bundesgesundheitsblatt 1989, No 1. Page 30f.

5 Damaschke, Sabine/Scheffer, Bernadette: Apotheken. Planen, Gestalten und Einrichten. Leinfelden-Echterdingen 2000.

6 DIN 277-1: 2005-02, Grundflächen und Rauminhalte von Bauwerken im Hochbau – Part 1: Begriffe, Ermittlungsgrundlagen | DIN 277- 2; 2005- 02, Grundflächen und Rauminhalte von Bauwerken im Hochbau – Part 2: Gliederung der Netto-Grundfläche [Nutzflächen, Technische Funktionsflächen und Verkehrsflächen] | DIN 277-3; 2005-04, Grundflächen und Rauminhalte von Bauwerken im Hochbau – Part 3: Mengen und Bezugseinheiten

7 DIN 13080: 2003-07, Gliederung des Krankenhauses in Funktionsbereiche und Funktionsstellen | Supplementary sheet 1: 2003-07, Gliederung des Krankenhauses in Funktionsbereiche und Funktionsstellen – Hinweise zur Anwendung für Allgemeine Krankenhäuser | Supplementary sheet 2: 2003- 07, Gliederung des Krankenhauses in Funktionsbereiche und Funktionsstellen – Hinweise zur Anwendung für Hochschul- und Universitätskliniken | Supplementary sheet 3: 1999-10, Gliederung des Krankenhauses in Funktionsbereiche und Funktionsstellen – Formblatt zur Ermittlung von Flächen im Krankenhaus | Supplementary sheet 4: 2004- 07, Gliederung des Krankenhauses in Funktionsbereiche und Funktionsstellen – Begriffe und Gliederung der Zielplanung für Allgemeine Krankenhäuser

8 Spegg, Horst: Apothekenbesichtigung. Ein Handbuch zur Selbstkontrolle des Apothekenbetriebs. Bearbeitet von Michael Schmidt. Stuttgart 2000.

9 DIN 12924-4: 1994-01, Laboreinrichtungen; Abzüge; Abzüge in Apotheken; Hauptmaße, Anforderungen und Prüfungen

10 Verordnung über Arbeitsstätten [Arbeitsstättenverordnung – ArbStättV], Bundesgesetzblatt I. Page 1595

11 DIN 276-1: 2006-11, Kosten im Bauwesen – Part 1: Hochbau

12 DIN 4109: 1989-11, Schallschutz im Hochbau; Anforderungen und Nachweise [will be revised in DIN 4109-1: 2006-10]

13 DIN 4102-1: 1998-05, Brandverhalten von Baustoffen und Bauteilen – Part 1: Baustoffe; Begriffe, Anforderungen und Prüfungen

14 DIN 5035-8: 2007-07, Beleuchtung mit künstlichem Licht – Part 8: Arbeitsplatzleuchten – Anforderungen, Empfehlungen und Prüfung

15 Frieling, Heinrich: Farbe am Arbeitsplatz. Munich 1992.

16 Honorarordnung für Architekten und Ingenieure in its current version of 1 Januar 1996. Stuttgart/Berlin/Cologne 1995.

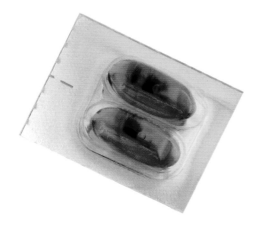

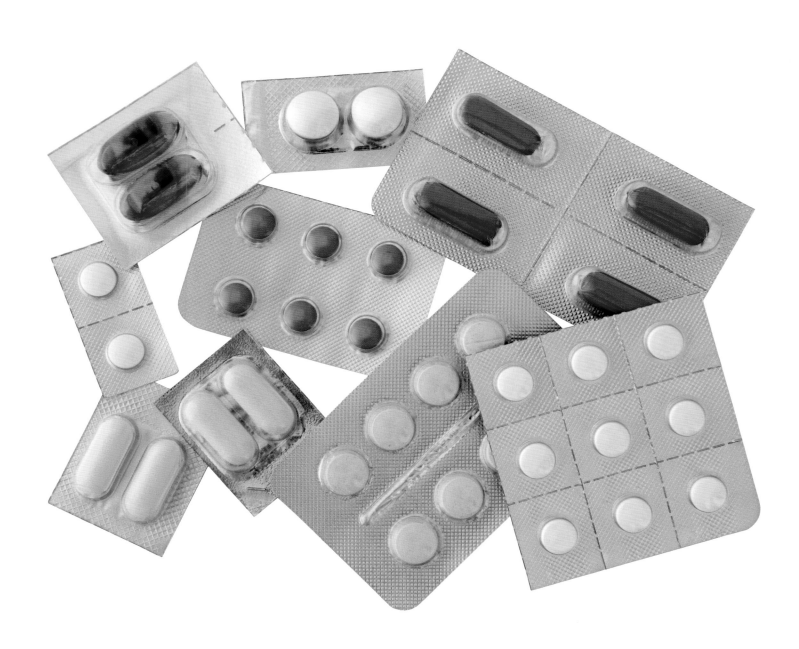

The Rheinstein-Apotheke, located in a new health center, has white fitted furniture and bold red, orange, lilac, and blue accents. The low budget involved, and the location alongside the front display window, posed a particular challenge for the architects: The pharmacy needed to look bright and modern while conveying gravitas and professional expertise.

Colour coding was used to create a simple and attractive product display, visible for the entire length of the store through floor-level windows. Indirectly lit shelves set into the wall add horizontal emphasis, while the plexiglass shelf signage uses the same system of colours to distinguish between different product categories and make the display more attractive.

The wall of shelves extends behind the angled cash desk, providing space for behind-the-counter products and also forming the entrance to the private areas of the pharmacy. Here, the entire front wall is dominated by a brightly coloured alphabetic storage drawer unit. There is also an assay area, work desks, a prescription area, and a controlled drug storage area. The screened-off stairs lead to the upstairs office, kitchen, and lounge for night staff.

**A-BASE
ARCHITECTS**

RHEINSTEIN-APOTHEKE
BERLIN | G

URBAN PHARMACY

MEDIUM-SIZED
PHARMACY

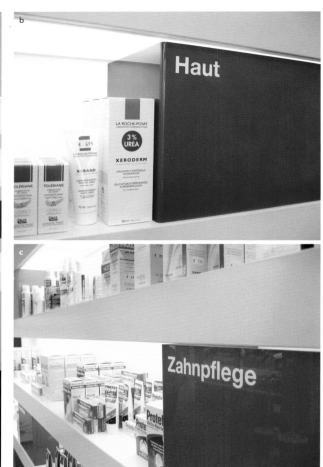

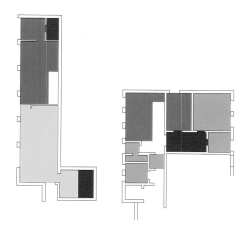

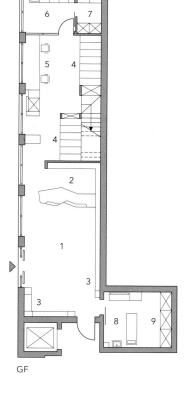

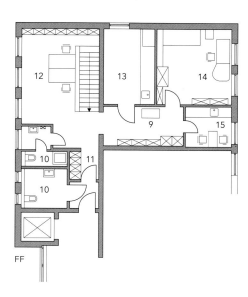

GF

FF

Client	operator	Kirsten Wieker
Design phase	10 2004–12 2004
Built	12 2004–01 2005
Gross floor area	205 sqm
Usable surface	172 sqm
Gross volume	716 cbm
Construction cost	90,000 €
Total cost	90,000 €

a The shelves set into the wall add horizontal emphasis to the space.
b Each group of products has its own plexiglass sign.
c Indirect lighting shows off the products to their best advantage.
d The pharmacy's effect is achieved using white fitted furniture and bold accents of colour.

Diagrammatic plans, to scale 1:400
Floor plans, to scale 1:200

Floor layout

1	Sales area	**6**	Prescription area	**11**	Staff changing
2	Cash desk	**7**	Drug storage	**12**	Office
3	Self-service area	**8**	Consultations	**13**	Laboratory
4	Alphabetic storage	**9**	Product storage	**14**	Night shift room
5	Workstation	**10**	Bathroom	**15**	Kitchen

The pharmacy is on two stories, with the upstairs laboratory and storage accessed via a single central flight of stairs or an outside elevator. The storage area in the consulting room is inconveniently located.

Usable areas

Sales	**yellow**	46 sqm	27 %
Service	**red**	48 sqm	28 %
Administration	**green**	19 sqm	11 %
Employee areas	**orange**	38 sqm	22 %
Supply	disposal	**brown**	21 sqm	12 %
Total		172 sqm	100 %

Other key information

Catchment radius	Not known
Distance to nearest pharmacy	
Nearest health facility	
Number of items in stock	
Stock turnover rate	
Proportion produced in-house	
Drugs produced in-house	
Proportion delivered externally	
Type of customers supplied	
Number of staff	
Prescriptions filled per day	
Proportion of special services	
Technical facilities	
Nature of special services	

This unusual pharmacy, with its large exposed concrete roof, is a dispensary, event space and herb garden all in one. The two-story building is located on a long, narrow site with streets on either side, in the center of the Aspern district of Vienna. It has to allow as much light as possible to reach the houses on both sides, and therefore has large front and back windows and a fully glazed atrium, complete with gingko tree. The bright, transparent look is enhanced by the shelves hanging from the concrete ceiling in the sales area, which do not touch the polished asphalt floor. The slightly offset rows of shelves, which are lit from the insides and to which the ceiling strip lights form a visual continuation, add tension and rhythm to this large space.

Each shelf has its own consultation area, which in turn adjoins the full-length drugs cabinet. The contrast between white furniture and grey concrete is one of the defining features of this interior. The dispensing area and a large seminar room are located at the rear of the first floor, and there is a medicinal herb garden on the roof terrace.

ARTEC ARCHITEKTEN

APOTHEKE "ZUM LÖWEN VON ASPERN"
VIENNA | A

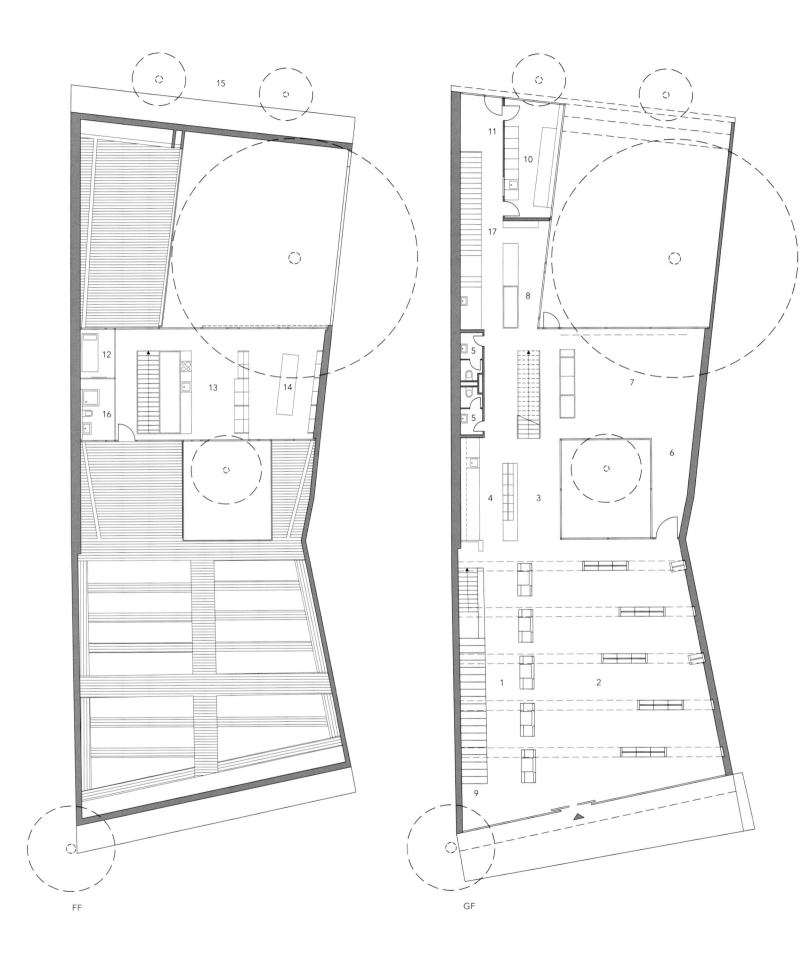

FF

GF

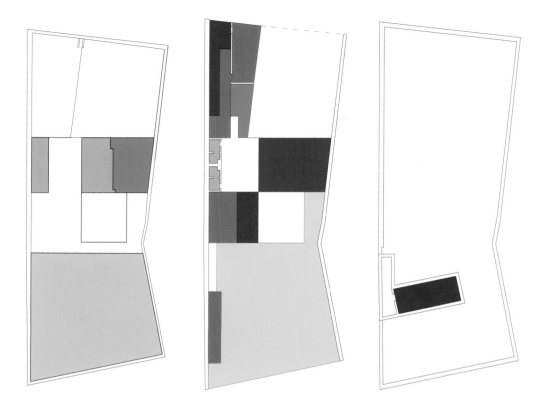

Diagrammatic plans, to scale 1:400
Floor plans, to scale 1:200

1 Sales area	**7** Seminar room	**13** Staff lounge
2 Self-service area	**8** Office	**14** Office
3 Drug storage	**9** Alphabetic storage	**15** Herb garden
4 Prescription area	**10** Laboratory	**16** Bathroom	shower
5 Bathroom	**11** Goods inwards	**17** Product storage
6 Consultations	**12** Night shift room	

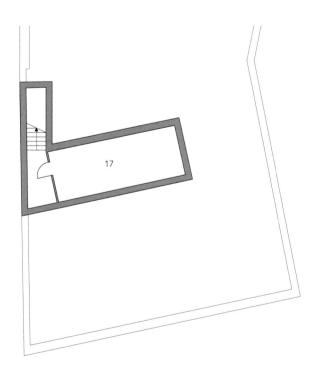

17

Client	operator	Wilhelm Schlagintweit
Design phase	10 2002 – 04 2003
Built	04 2003 – 09 2003
Gross floor area	581 sqm
Usable surface	464 sqm
Gross volume	2,500 cbm
Construction cost	1,000,000 €
Total cost	1,000,000 €

a Large windows overlook an atrium containing a gingko tree.

b The contrast between the white furniture and grey concrete is one of the interior's defining features.

c The striplights on the suspended shelves continue to the ceiling, creating a sense of tension and rhythm in this large space.

Floor layout

The pharmacy is on three floors, so staff have to do a considerable amount of walking around, but there are conveniently located stairs to the upstairs office and staff lounge and basement storage area. The consultation and seminar rooms in the courtyard and the rooftop herb garden work particularly well.

Usable areas

Sales	**yellow**	207 sqm	45 %
Service	**red**	67 sqm	14 %
Administration	**green**	41 sqm	9 %
Employee areas	**orange**	44 sqm	9 %
Supply	disposal	**brown**	55 sqm	12 %
Training	**violet**	50 sqm	11 %
Total		464 sqm	100 %

Other key information

Catchment radius	6 km
Distance to nearest pharmacy	500 m
Nearest health facility	Hospital, medical practice
Number of items in stock	6,500
Stock turnover rate	12
Number of staff	24
Prescriptions filled per day	250
Proportion of special services	10 %
Technical facilities	Air conditioner

Nature of special services: cosmetics, skin and face analysis, yoga, qigong, fasting cures, nutrition advice, cultural program, lectures

The redesigned Apotheke Süd is a model of simple saffron elegance. Located on the first floor of a new medical clinic, it posed something of an architectural challenge with only 263 square metres of available space, no partition walls, and fully glazed sides. It also needed to be divided into separate areas.

Full-height, double-sided wall storage units separate the sales area from the store windows and adjoining areas, creating a space within a space. The display space surrounds are inscribed with writing, a recurring detail throughout the pharmacy. They serve both as an indirect light source – they are lit by neon strips – and as a way of categorising the products. The backs of the wall storage units, which face the front window, are used for the window display and also protect the interior from bright sunlight.

A freestanding display unit in the middle of the sales area enhances the design and draws customers' attention to the counter placed diagonally at the end of the customer area and leading to the alphabetic storage cabinets. There is also a separate open-plan area.

**BPW
ARCHITEKTUR**

APOTHEKE SÜD
ST. PÖLTEN | A

NEW CONSTRUCTION

URBAN PHARMACY

MEDIUM-SIZED
PHARMACY

URB

MED

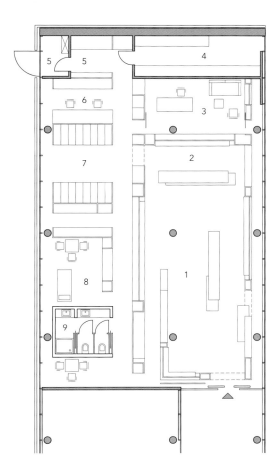

Client | operator	Johann Vogl	
Design phase	11 2003 – 02 2005	
Built	03 2005 – 07 2005	
Gross floor area	284 sqm	
Usable surface	263 sqm	
Gross volume	1,020 cbm	
Total cost	430,000 €	

a The redesigned pharmacy: simple,
   elegant, saffron.
b The counter is positioned diagonally at
   the end of the customer area.
c The gaps between the various displays
   create rhythm and variety.
d The backs of the wall units face the store
   window and are used for the window
   display.

Diagrammatic plans, to scale 1:400
Floor plans, to scale 1:200

Floor layout

1	Sales area	**4**	Product storage	**7**	Alphabetic storage
2	Cash desk	**5**	Goods inwards	**8**	Consultations
3	Office	**6**	Prescription area	**9**	Bathroom | shower

The highly structured floor plan contains all the areas normally found in a
pharmacy, with the exception of a laboratory. The layout has been designed
for maximum user friendliness, and includes a customer bathroom, but there
are no rest areas for staff.

Usable areas

Sales	**yellow**	122 sqm	46 %
Service	**red**	79 sqm	30 %
Administration	**green**	25 sqm	10 %
Employee areas	**orange**	8 sqm	3 %
Supply | disposal	**brown**	29 sqm	11 %
Total		263 sqm	100 %

Other key information

Catchment radius	5 km
Distance to nearest pharmacy	600 m
Number of items in stock	9,250
Stock turnover rate	12 %
Proportion produced in-house	under 1 %
Drugs produced in-house	Tinctures, inunction, salves
Type of customers supplied	Regular and walk-in customers
Number of staff	23/10, 29/10
Prescriptions filled per day	150
Technical facilities	Air conditioner

Nature of special services: cosmetics, blood pressure, and weight
measurements

Visitors enter the spacious customer area, which stretches almost for the full length of the space, though one of two entrances. The shelves on the side walls have been tapered inwards to make the walls look longer, giving an eyecatching view of the glass-fronted alphabetic storage unit at the end of the space. The long, relatively narrow sales area is lined with shelves on both sides, with the sides of the counters placed in front of it, creating a calm, relaxed feel.

The display and consultation counter in the customer service area at the entrance is used to advertise special offers and separate advice from sales. The adjoining counters allow staff to maintain visual contact with customers when using the alphabetic storage unit behind the glass wall. Gaps between the self-service shelves, which are ranged in front of a long aisle, provide easy access to the other areas of the building.

The pharmacy's colour scheme of graduated greys emphasises the width of this large space. The shape and colour of the monolithic-looking white Corian desks in the sales area make them stand out sharply from their surroundings, contrasting with the rest of the largely linear design.

BPW ARCHITEKTUR

VITAL APOTHEKE
VIENNA | A

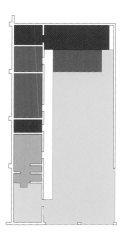

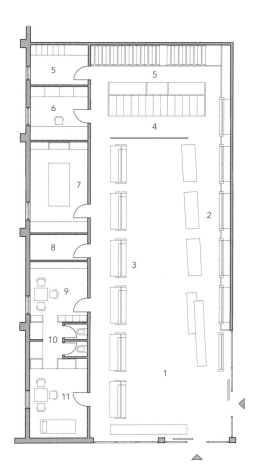

Client	operator	Marcel Mathà
Design phase	2003
Built	08 2004 – 11 2004
Gross floor area	260 sqm
Usable surface	238 sqm
Gross volume	960 cbm
Total cost	420,000 €

a The glass-fronted alphabetic storage unit at the end of the long, narrow sales area.

b The shape and colour of the monolithic-looking white Corian desks in the sales area make them stand out sharply from their surroundings, contrasting with the otherwise linear design.

Diagrammatic plans, to scale 1:400
Floor plans, to scale 1:200

Floor layout

1 Sales area	5 Product storage	9 Staff lounge
2 Cash desk	6 Prescription area	10 Bathroom
3 Self-service area	7 Laboratory	11 Consultations
4 Alphabetic storage	8 Storage	

The layout of the rooms on the rectangular site reflects their functions. Separate access was needed for goods being delivered to the storage and alphabetic storage area, and customers have easy access to a conveniently located bathroom. There is no office or rest area for night staff.

Usable areas

Sales	**yellow**	145 sqm	61 %
Service	**red**	41 sqm	17 %
Employee areas	**orange**	18 sqm	8 %
Supply	disposal	**brown**	34 sqm	14 %
Total		238 sqm	100 %

Other key information

Catchment radius	0,6 km
Distance to nearest pharmacy	630 m
Nearest health facility	Retirement home, medical practice
Number of items in stock	6,000
Stock turnover rate	15
Proportion produced in-house	0,01 %
Drugs produced in-house	Teas, disinfectants, addictive drugs, vitamins, cosmetics
Proportion delivered externally	5 %
Number of staff	6 Full time, 6 Part time
Prescriptions filled per day	250
Proportion of special services	3 %
Technical facilities	Air conditioner

Nature of special services: blood and vascular measurement, cosmetics, facial analysis, information evenings

The massive curved concrete counter in the middle of the Adler Apotheke provides an eyecatching sculptural centerpiece. Its monolithic elegance also symbolises durability and reliability, but also dynamism, movement, and kinetic energy. It is nine metres long, made from a single piece of concrete and curves diagonally through the interior with a depth of up to 120 centimetre, resembling a sinuous plesiosaur. The counter will undoubtedly remain in position for many decades, its immutability a reminder that despite the pharmacy's new location, it has a 100-year history.

The space is strongly horizontal, with curving timber-clad walls, veneered cylindrical columns and glass steles in the display window. The dark Wenge wood horizontal wall cladding accentuates and frames the red-backlit shelves. The dramatic colours and lines contrast with the simple materials of the interior, which is dominated by Wenge wood, slate, and concrete.

The pharmacy has two stories: the lower with the alphabetic storage area and controlled drug storage at the rear, and the upper, accessed via an internal staircase, containing the office, prescription area, and staff lounge.

JÖRN BATHKE

ADLER APOTHEKE
KAMEN | G

URBAN PHARMACY

MEDIUM-SIZED
PHARMACY

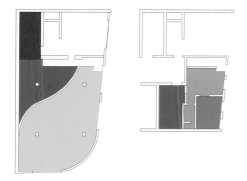

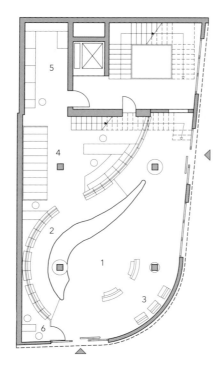

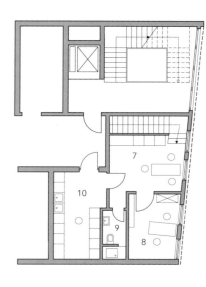

Client | operator Eva Rapos
Design phase | built 2007
Usable surface 163 sqm
Gross volume 584 cbm
Total cost 168,000 €

a The nine-metre counter, shaped from a single piece of concrete, curves diagonally though the space.
b The dark Wenge wood horizontal wall cladding accentuates the red-backlit shelves.

Diagrammatic plans, to scale 1:400
Floor plans, to scale 1:200

Floor layout

1	Sales area	**5**	Drug storage	**9**	Bathroom	shower
2	Cash desk	**6**	Consultations	**10**	Prescription area	
3	Self-service area	**7**	Staff lounge		laboratory
4	Alphabetic storage	**8**	Office		

The two-story building has some shortcomings: The combined prescription area and laboratory on the upper floor are accessible only via a staircase, though this is less important in the case of the office and lounge. Likewise, access to the office via the staff lounge is less than ideal.

Usable areas

Sales	**yellow**	81 sqm	50 %
Service	**red**	40 sqm	25 %
Administration	**green**	11 sqm	7 %
Employee areas	**orange**	17 sqm	10 %
Supply	disposal	**brown**	14 sqm	8 %
Total		163 sqm	100 %

Other key information

Catchment radius	10 km
Distance to nearest pharmacy	150 m
Nearest health facility	Medical houses, medical practice
Proportion produced in-house	1 %
Drugs produced in-house	Salves, tinctures
Proportion delivered externally	15 %
Type of customers supplied	Retirement homes
Number of staff	6
Technical facilities	Air conditioner, laboratory facilities

Nature of special services: blood pressure, blood sugar, and cholesterol testing, compression stockings, baby weighing-scale, and inhaler loans, prescription pickup service, cosmetics training

The modern Wilhelm Apotheke lies behind a Stalinist precast concrete-slab façade on Berlin's historic Wilhelmstraße. Specialising in traditional Chinese medicine, it also uses the Normamed® system and detailed patient case histories.

The interior design is intended to bridge the gap between mainstream European medicine and complementary Asian therapies. The strict rectangular floorplan contrasts with the gently rounded counter. The counters are surrounded by colourful cylindrical columns decorated with specially made, digitally printed, and enlarged motifs from traditional Chinese medicine. Horizontal plywood sheets are fitted to the semicircular wall separating the sales area from the offices, with narrow tubular aluminum spacers being used to create an attractive light and shade effect.

The counters, too, have been designed to make an impression, with small LED lights shining through the translucent green countertops. These create an enigmatic impression of depth and contrast effectively with the dark matt surfaces of the furnishings.

JÖRN BATHKE

WILHELM APOTHEKE
BERLIN | G

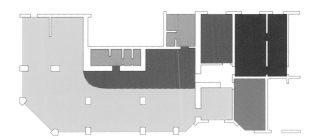

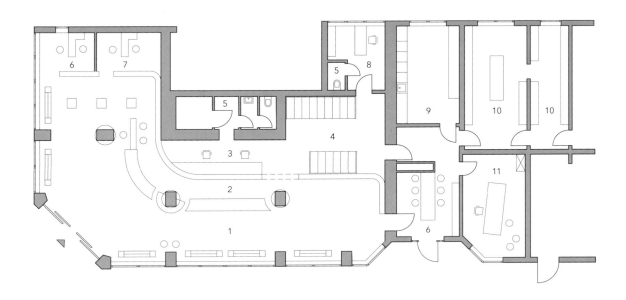

Client | operator   Christian Melzer
Design phase | built   2006
Usable surface   306 sqm
Gross volumet   801 cbm
Total cost   230,000 €

a Horizontal plywood panels create an
    attractive chiaroscuro effect.
b Small LED lights shine through the trans-
    lucent green countertops.
c Brightly coloured cylindrical columns
    surround the counters.

Diagrammatic plans, to scale 1:400
Floor plans, to scale 1:200

Floor layout

1 Sales area	**5** Bathroom	**9** Prescription area |
2 Cash desk	**6** Consultations	laboratory
3 Workstation	**7** Private consultations	**10** Product storage
4 Alphabetic storage	**8** Night shift room	**11** Office

This single-story pharmacy has been designed for maximum user friendliness. There are three consultation rooms, one with additional outside access, but the staff lounge is too small.

Usable areas

Sales	**yellow**	162 sqm	53 %
Service	**red**	59 sqm	19 %
Administration	**green**	21 sqm	7 %
Employee areas	**orange**	22 sqm	7 %
Supply | disposal	**brown**	42 sqm	14 %
Total		306 sqm	100 %

Other key information

Catchment radius	50 km
Distance to nearest pharmacy	300 m
Nearest health facility	Medical practice
Number of items in stock	4,000
Stock turnover rate	12
Proportion produced in-house	2 %
Drugs produced in-house	TCM
Proportion delivered externally	0 %
Number of staff	4
Proportion of special services	10 %
Nature of special services	TCM

Although there are relatively few pharmacies in Berlin's working-class district of Wedding, it is still difficult to set up a new one. The newly built DocPlus-Apotheke has succeeded, thanks to a combination of low prices and a bright, well-lit environment.

Full-size windows make the long, narrow sales area on the ground floor clearly visible from outside, encouraging passers-by to enter the store. The wave-shaped counters and self-service areas behind this extend almost the full length of the space, ending with a spiral staircase to the upstairs offices and basement storage and bathroom. Strip lighting on the ceiling guides visitors towards the additional rear exit, improving the customer flow and connecting the pharmacy to other shops and a parking area.

The interior is dominated by pale white and by highly grained Zebrano wood. Monitors above the counter are used to advertise special offers, and the backlit self-service displays encourage customers to take a closer look.

BRANDHERM +KRUMREY

DOCPLUS-APOTHEKE
BERLIN | G

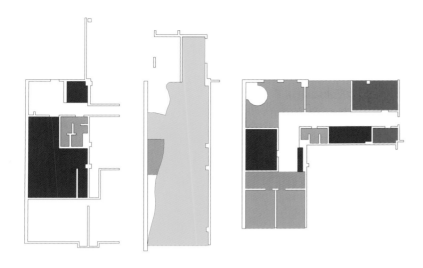

Diagrammatic plans, to scale 1:400
Floor plans, to scale 1:200

1	Sales area	**6**	Server room	**10**	Staff changing
2	Counters	**7**	Laboratory |	**11**	Staff lounge
3	Self-service area		prescription area	**12**	Night shift room
4	Workstation	**8**	Bathroom | shower	**13**	Product storage
5	Consultations	**9**	Order picker	**14**	Bathroom

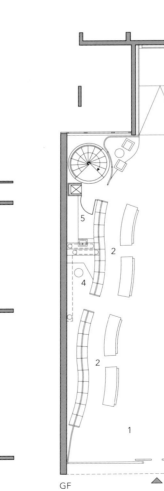

BSMT

GF

FF

Client	operator	Axel Müller-de Ahna
Design phase	06 2007
Built	07 2007–12 2007
Gross floor area	396 sqm
Usable surface	342 sqm

a The wave-shaped counters extend almost the full length of the space.
b The interior is dominated by pale whites and highly grained Zebrano wood.
c Monitors are used to advertise special offers.
d Strip lights on the ceiling guide customers towards the rear of the store.
e The backlit motif on the self-service display helps to create a pleasant atmosphere.

Floor layout

The customer areas and a small office are located on the first floor. All other rooms are upstairs and in the basement. There is also a small goods lift and a conveyor belt from the automated stockroom.

Usable areas

Sales	**yellow**	124 sqm	36 %
Service	**red**	23 sqm	7 %
Employee areas	**orange**	109 sqm	32 %
Supply | disposal	**brown**	86 sqm	25 %
Total		342 sqm	100 %

Other key information

Catchment radius	3 km
Distance to nearest pharmacy	200 m
Nearest health facility	Medical practice
Number of items in stock	12,000
Proportion produced in-house	0,5 %
Drugs produced in-house	Prescriptions
Proportion delivered externally	0,5 %
Type of customers supplied	Private clients
Number of staff	6
Technical facilities	Air conditioner
Nature of special services	Health care

The Einhorn Apotheke's unicorn logo extends prominently across almost the whole width of the counter. Outside, prominent red signage draws attention to the pharmacy, and accentuates the pilaster strips between the window axes on the somewhat jaded 1970s façade.

Inside, red is also used as a means of communication: The curved rear wall creates a sense of continuity within the sales area and separates it visually from those areas not accessible to the public, while the dark, restrained colour of the counter stands in pleasant contrast, adding a calm, elegant feel to the space. Simple white surfaces have been used in the self-service area, with the dark tone serving as a grounding element for the shelves used to store excess stock.

The dispensary at the back of the room has been designed for visibility, and is separated from the customer area by a glass wall. There are no fewer than three conveniently positioned customer entrances, plus an additional one for goods deliveries.

BRANDHERM +KRUMREY

EINHORN APOTHEKE
HAMBURG | G

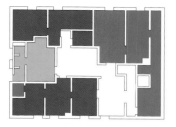

BSMT

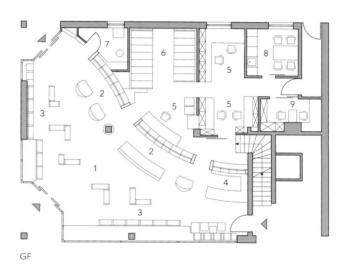

GF

Client	operator	Hella Dierking
Design phase	03 2004 – 10 2004
Built	10 2004 – 01 2005
Usable surface	302 sqm
Gross volume	900 cbm

a The unicorn logo stands prominently above the sales counter.
b Simple white surfaces have been used in the self-service area.
c The red sales counter has a slot that dispenses receipts.
d The dispensary at the back of the store is designed with visibility in mind.

Diagrammatic plans, to scale 1:400
Floor plans, to scale 1:200

Floor layout

1	Sales area	**5**	Workstation	**10**	Product storage
2	Cash desk | behind-the-counter shelves	**6**	Alphabetic storage	**11**	Plant room
3	Self-service area	**7**	Consultations	**12**	Staff changing
4	Prescription area	**8**	Staff lounge	**13**	Bathroom
		9	Office	**14**	Laboratory

In this two-story pharmacy, the customer area is located very close to the private sections of the building. The laboratory, staff changing rooms, and storage space are in the basement.

Usable areas

Sales	**yellow**	91 sqm	30 %
Service	**red**	73 sqm	24 %
Administration	**green**	6 sqm	2 %
Employee areas	**orange**	28 sqm	9 %
Supply | disposal	**brown**	66 sqm	22 %
Plant	**blue**	38 sqm	13 %
Total		302 sqm	100 %

Other key information

Catchment radius	5 km
Distance to nearest pharmacy	200 m
Nearest health facility	Clinic, medical practice
Technical facilities	Air conditioner

Nature of special services: endocrinology advice, cosmetics

The Malteser Apotheke is located in a former working-class district of Duisburg, close to one of several harbors used to load coal from the Ruhr. The pharmacy's interior emphasises its historic past with large backlit photographs of the port, extending in a band all the way round the sales area.

When the pharmacy was redesigned, the intention was to increase the sales area and foster a more contemporary image. The use of a space-saving stock picker in the basement meant that the storage drawers in the dispensary were no longer required and the sales areas could be opened up to the display window. This increased the available space by about 40 square metres.

A diagonal sales counter with high shelves behind it conceals the entrance to the basement, its striking rust-red colour serving as an eye-catching feature in its own right. Two smaller counters stand opposite this, forming a second sales unit which can be used for more detailed consultations. Colour is used to separate the two areas visually and provide guidance, with the rust-red being replaced by a low-key pale blue in the consultation area.

BRANDHERM +KRUMREY

MALTESER APOTHEKE
DUISBURG | G

Top Angebot!

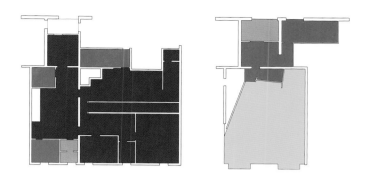

Diagrammatic plans, to scale 1:400
Floor plans, to scale 1:200

1	Sales area	**8**	Staff lounge | night shift room
2	Cash desk		
3	Self-service area	**9**	Prescription area | laboratory
4	Behind-the-counter shelves		
		10	Goods inwards
5	Workstation	**11**	Plant room
6	Consultations	**12**	Bathroom
7	Product storage	**13**	Product storage

14	Prescription
15	Dispatch
16	Order picker
17	Kitchen | laundry
18	Conveyors
19	Server room

URB

LAR

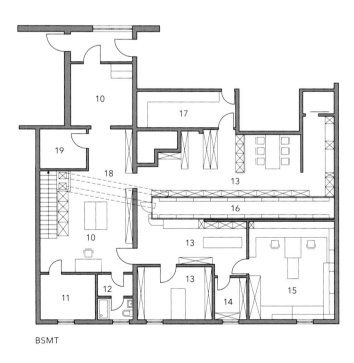

BSMT

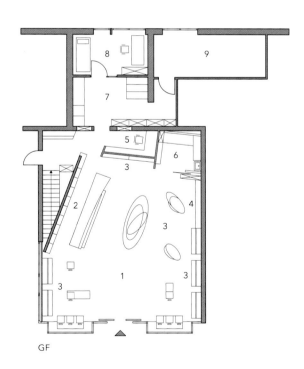

GF

**Client	operator**	Georg Kuchler
Design phase	02 2006 – 06 2006
Built	07 2006 – 09 2006
Gross floor area	370 sqm
Usable surface	331 sqm

a The diagonal open-display counter conceals the entrance to the basement.

b In the self-service area, the rust-red that dominates the open display area is replaced by a subdued light blue.

c Two smaller counters are used to provide more detailed advice to customers.

d Full-height frosted glass sliding doors separate the consultation area from the rest of the pharmacy.

e The self-service area, with one of the backlit local photographs

Floor layout

The fact that the pharmacy is on two floors involves considerable comings and goings of people and materials, and there is only one staircase, on the edge of the building. Most of the materials handling takes place downstairs; some of the rooms here are windowless and thus air-conditioned. There is a service area, an employee lounge, and a bathroom, but no office.

Usable areas

Sales	**yellow**	87 sqm	26 %
Service	**red**	57 sqm	17 %
Employee areas	**orange**	16 sqm	5 %
Supply	disposal	**brown**	162 sqm	49 %
Plant	**blue**	9 sqm	3 %
Total		331 sqm	100 %

Other key information

Catchment radius	10 km
Distance to nearest pharmacy	200 m
Nearest health facility	Medical practice
Number of items in stock	10,000
Stock turnover rate	14
Proportion produced in-house	under 1 %
Drugs produced in-house	Medical regulations
Technical facilities	Air conditioner, order picker, conveyors, elevators

Nature of special services: makeup studio, health-food café
[Self-help, customer club]

The new Alpin Apotheke is located in a medical center close to a hospital in the Allgäu mountains, and a picture of the surrounding landscape is displayed above the shelves extending along the whole length of the sales counter. Local materials such as sycamore and slate have been used in an expression of the young pharmacist's love of the area and of the natural environment, which is also reflected in the name of the business.

Two other fundamental themes of the design are openness and transparency. The large, open-plan sales area is visible at a glance, and the dispensary is separated from it only by a glass screen. Movable display shelves have been placed in front of the full-height windows facing the street, their small size allowing an ample view of the interior to lure passers-by inside.

The sense of openness is increased by the use of simple, uniform materials: a green slate floor in the public area and sycamore parquet in the staff-only parts of the building. One unusual feature of this pharmacy, perhaps a foretaste of the future, is a drive-in counter.

KLAUS R. BÜRGER   **ALPIN APOTHEKE AM KLINIKUM**
KEMPTEN | G

URBAN PHARMACY

MEDIUM-SIZED
PHARMACY

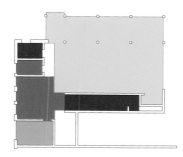

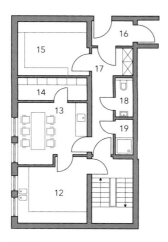

BSMT

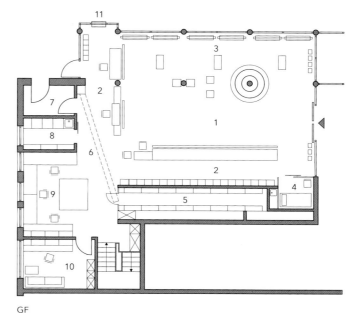

GF

Client | operator   Michael Bentz
Design phase | built   2006
Usable surface   236 sqm

a Movable display shelves have been positioned in front of the full-height store windows.
b The bench in the middle of the pharmacy provides a splash of bright colour.
c The spacious, open-plan sales area makes an immediate impact on visitors.
d A picture of the surrounding mountains extends the full length of the counter.

Diagrammatic plans, to scale 1:400
Floor plans, to scale 1:200

Floor layout

1	Sales area	**8**	Prescription area	**14**	Staff changing
2	Cash desk	**9**	Workstation	**15**	Product storage
3	Self-service area	**10**	Night shift room	**16**	Sluice
4	Consultations	**11**	Night shift desk | drive-in	**17**	Server room
5	Product storage			**18**	Bathroom
6	Conveyors	**12**	Laboratory	**19**	Shower
7	Goods inwards	**13**	Staff lounge		

The pharmacy's very concentrated floor plan, with almost no aisles, makes it very user friendly. The automated stockroom reduces the amount of space required, and there is even a drive-in night counter.

Usable areas

Sales	**yellow**	117 sqm	50 %
Service	**red**	43 sqm	18 %
Specialist areas	**pink**	4 sqm	2 %
Employee areas	**orange**	34 sqm	14 %
Supply | disposal	**brown**	34 sqm	14 %
Plant	**blue**	4 sqm	2 %
Total		236 sqm	100 %

Other key information

Catchment radius	20 km
Distance to nearest pharmacy	800 m
Nearest health facility	Medical practice
Number of items in stock	6,500
Drugs produced in-house	Teas, Bach flowers, vitamins
Number of staff	6 Full time, 3 Part time
Prescriptions filled per day	81
Technical facilities	Air conditioner, order picker, conveyors

Nature of special services: facial analysis, travel medicine, aromatherapy, free delivery, cosmetic studio, blister packaging, footcare practice, own brand under development

URB

MED

Less is more in the new interior and exterior of the pharmacy on Klemensplatz in Düsseldorf. The futuristic, simply laid-out dispensary is almost all white, with only a few strategically positioned display surfaces. A deliberate decision has been made to have no self-service area, thus placing the entire focus on the pharmacist and her team. There are no in-your-face Buy Me signs, no overflowing shelves, and all is pure form and function.

A wide counter made from dark cherrywood seems to float above its two simple metal feet, dominating the minimalist sales area. A small, simple shelf has been placed in front of the full-height display window to avoid obstructing the view from outside. At the back of the sales area a frosted glass screen, used to display the small number of behind-the-counter products, separates the tea dispensary, which is not accessible to customers. A consultation booth stands at the interface of the public and private areas, creating transparency between the two and saving space for workstations.

KLAUS R. BÜRGER   **APOTHEKE AM KLEMENSPLATZ**
DÜSSELDORF | G

URBAN PHARMACY

MEDIUM-SIZED
PHARMACY

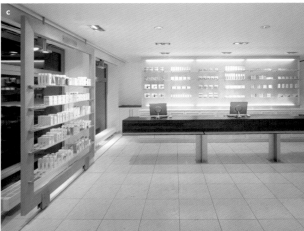

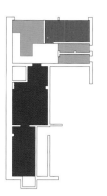
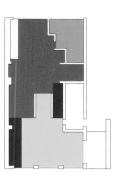

BSMT

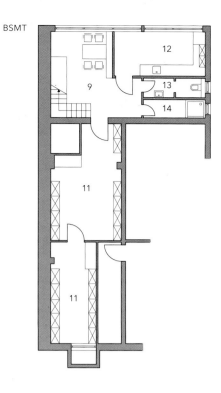

GF

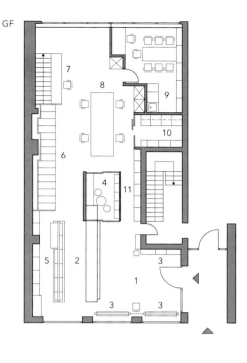

Client | operator	Karin Waldmann
Design phase	03 2003 – 02 2004
Built	02 2004 – 04 2004
Gross floor area	216 sqm
Usable surface	197 sqm
Gross volume	605 cbm
Construction cost	286,000 €
Total cost	398,000 €

a The sales area contains a small number of judiciously positioned displays.
b The wide, dark cherrywood counter
c The simple, futuristic sales area
d The consultation booth between the public and private areas
e Workstations at the back of the pharmacy

Diagrammatic plans, to scale 1:400
Floor plans, to scale 1:200

Floor layout

1	Sales area	**6**	Alphabetic storage	**11**	Product storage
2	Cash desk	**7**	Dispatch	**12**	Laboratory
3	Self-service area	**8**	Workstation	**13**	Bathroom
4	Consultations	**9**	Staff lounge	**14**	Shower
5	Tea-prescription area	**10**	Prescription area		

The space on the first floor is designed to be simple and functional. There is a soundproofed consulting room for customers, and two rest areas for staff. The laboratory, storage, and staff rooms are in the basement, reached via a single flight of stairs.

Usable areas

Sales	**yellow**	42 sqm	21 %
Service	**red**	76 sqm	39 %
Employee areas	**orange**	35 sqm	18 %
Supply | disposal	**brown**	44 sqm	22 %
Total		197 sqm	100 %

Other key information

Catchment radius	8 km
Distance to nearest pharmacy	300 m
Nearest health facility	none
Number of items in stock	17,500
Stock turnover rate	10,5 months
Proportion produced in-house	5 %
Drugs produced in-house	Capsules, salves, teas, cosmetics
Proportion delivered externally	20 %
Number of staff	7
Technical facilities	Air conditioner

Nature of special services: prescription collection, home delivery, preventive health (blood pressure, blood sugar, and cholesterol testing, body structure analysis), nutritional advice, seminars, walking courses, specialist makeup advice, compression stocking fitting, incontinence advice, vaccinations, travel medicine.

URB

MED

This pharmacy, dating from 1952, has been renovated several times. The latest redesign required great sensitivity and a reduction to the essentials. The historic street-corner building is only 112 square metres in area, and making it look bigger required a degree of imagination.

The red pharmacy logo in the windows is echoed in the movable partition in front of the alphabetic storage unit and consulting room, whose gleaming surface is clearly visible from outside the store. The absence of a window display, an increasingly common trend in today's pharmacies, turns the interior into an eyecatching advertisement for itself.

The design uses a careful balance of materials in which each detail has a counterpart: for example the self-service shelves are attached to the wall by invisible fixings, while the behind-the-counter shelves are linked by a steel cable structure. In this fine piece of symbolism, in one area customers can freely choose what they buy, whereas in the other their decision is guided by the pharmacist.

Likewise, the heavy counter conveys a message of stolid reliability, while the brightly lit shelving system looks more lightweight and cheerful. And in one other welcoming detail, the screen fixings incorporate filigree vases of flowers.

KLAUS R. BÜRGER   **BURG APOTHEKE**
GREFRATH–OEDT | G

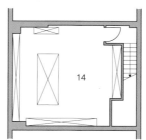

Client | operator   Axel Schulte
Design phase | built   2004
Usable surface   141 sqm

a The red pharmacists' logo in the window
has its chromatic counterpart in the movable partition in front of the alphabetic
storage area.
b The behind-the-counter shelves are
linked by steel cables.
c The absence of a window display lures the
eye into the interior of the pharmacy.

Diagrammatic plans, to scale 1:400
Floor plans, to scale 1:200

Floor layout

1	Sales area	**6**	Alphabetic storage		shift room
2	Cash desk	**7**	Workstation	**12**	Bathroom | shower
3	Behind-the-counter	**8**	Prescription area	**13**	Kitchen
	shelves	**9**	Goods inwards	**14**	Product storage
4	Self-service area	**10**	Laboratory		
5	Consultations	**11**	Staff lounge | night		

The different areas have been cleverly arranged on a long, narrow site.
The storage is in the basement, and the lounge and night workers' room
is also used as an office.

Usable areas

Sales	**yellow**	37 sqm	26 %
Service	**red**	44 sqm	31 %
Employee areas	**orange**	18 sqm	13 %
Supply | disposal	**brown**	42 sqm	30 %
Total		141 sqm	100 %

Other key information

Catchment radius	3–7 km
Distance to nearest pharmacy	500 m
Nearest health facility	Medical practice
Number of items in stock	3,000
Proportion produced in-house	5 %
Drugs produced in-house	Salves, cremes, suppositorien, solution
Type of customers supplied	Retirement homes, nursing service, private clients
Number of staff	3/3
Proportion of special services	5 %
Technical facilities	Air conditioner

Nature of special services: geriatric pharmacy, pharmaceutical care,
pharmacy shop, delivery service

RUR

SMA

A bright orange pharmacy? Despite, or perhaps because of his low budget, the young pharmacist wanted an offbeat, spacious interior with a small number of distinctive fittings and bold shapes and colours.

The spacious and impressive shop, located in a former industrial building, certainly lent itself to an unusual design. The visible joists and large shop window set the esthetic tone for the whole pharmacy, with the open-plan, generously proportioned loft-like space being preserved by the renovation. This is underlined by the hardwearing industrial oak parquet, but the most prominent feature of the interior is the bright orange concave semicircular counter, its front decorated with pharmacy-related words. The colourful counter near the entrance, a few steps below the sales area, is equally impressive. The fittings are made using exhibition stand technology, a flexible, low-cost solution. In a further elegant detail, the countertop surface is orange leather.

KLAUS R. BÜRGER   **OHM-APOTHEKE**
ERLANGEN | G

sts. physiologisch-chemische untersuchungen.
nische pharmazie. biochemie. ernährung. ohm
elle chinesische medizin. ohm apotheke.

UPB

LAB

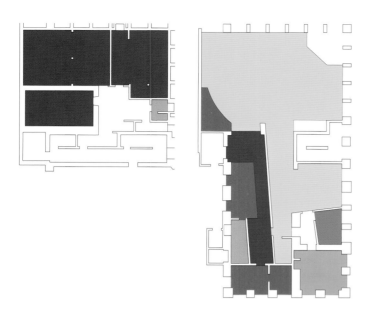

1 Sales area	**7** Product storage	**13** Consultations
2 Cash desk	**8** Workstation	**14** Private
3 Self-service area	**9** Kitchen | staff	consultations
4 Behind-the-counter	lounge	**15** Office
shelves	**10** Product storage	**16** Night shift room |
5 Workstation	**11** Laboratory	office
6 Goods inwards	**12** Prescription area	**17** Bathroom

URB

BSMT

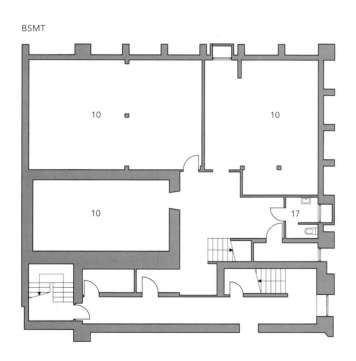

GF

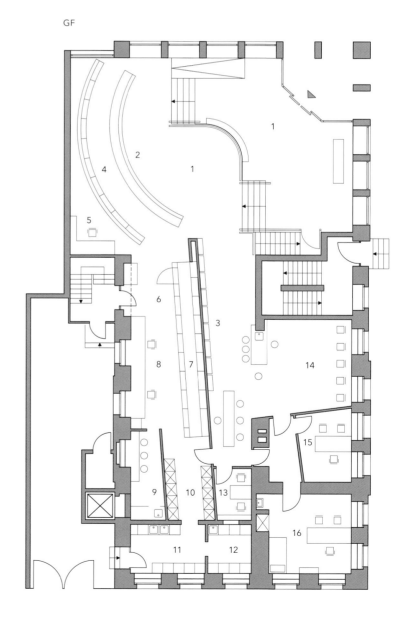

Diagrammatic plans, to scale 1:400
Floor plans, to scale 1:200

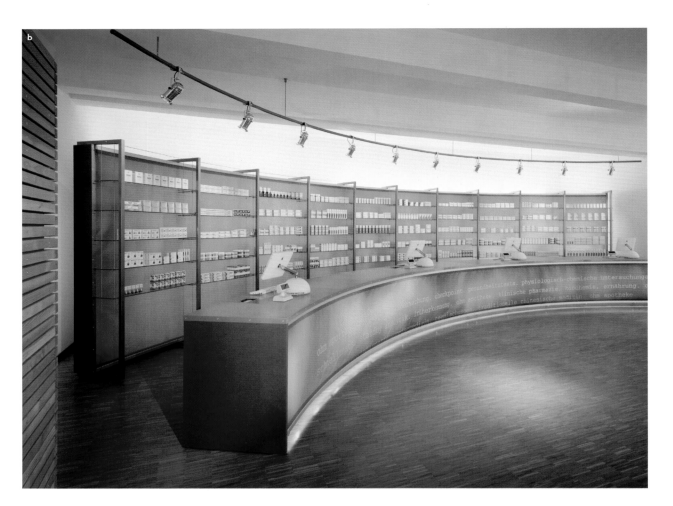

Client | operator	Ingo Deinl
Design phase | built	2004
Gross floor area	539 sqm
Usable surface	495 sqm
Gross volume	2,156 cbm

a All of the shop fittings are made using ex-
hibition-stand technology.
b The concave semicircular counter is the
most eye-catching feature of the interior.
c Bright orange is the dominant colour in
the spacious sales area.

Floor layout

The pharmacy has plenty of space spread over two levels, and the customer area is unusually large. The equally expansive basement stockrooms are accessed from the first floor via a staircase.

Usable areas

Sales	**yellow**	221 sqm	45 %
Service	**red**	68 sqm	14 %
Administration	**green**	12 sqm	2 %
Employee areas	**orange**	14 sqm	3 %
Supply | disposal	**brown**	180 sqm	36 %
Total		495 sqm	100 %

Other key information

Catchment radius	Not known
Distance to nearest pharmacy	
Nearest health facility	
Number of items in stock	
Stock turnover rate	
Proportion produced in-house	
Drugs produced in-house	
Proportion delivered externally	
Type of customers supplied	
Number of staff	
Prescriptions filled per day	
Proportion of special services	
Nature of special services	

The large number of pillars in the redesigned pharmacy, which was previously located next door, reflects the combination of old and new fabric. The existing building was expanded to create a 175-square-metre space.

Visitors entering via the two semicircular steps can see deep into the building. Its generous size is underlined by two long counters, each with three cash desks, while the shelves at the back screen off the private areas of the pharmacy. A spiral staircase leads upstairs. The automated stockroom is located in an orange glass shell and lies at the rear of the pharmacy, visible through the store window and through a gap in the self-service shelves.

The large sales area is divided into several sections by mobile, slightly rounded shelves made from waxed grey fiber cement backplates with integral glass bases. Sealed oak cubes at the bases of the shelves are used to store excess stock, and both oak and fiber cement are also used in the counters. The seamless polished Bitu-Terrazzo asphalt screed floor serves as the link between the old and new parts of the building.

MICHAEL CLAASSEN

APOTHEKE SCHNAITH
BURGDORF | G

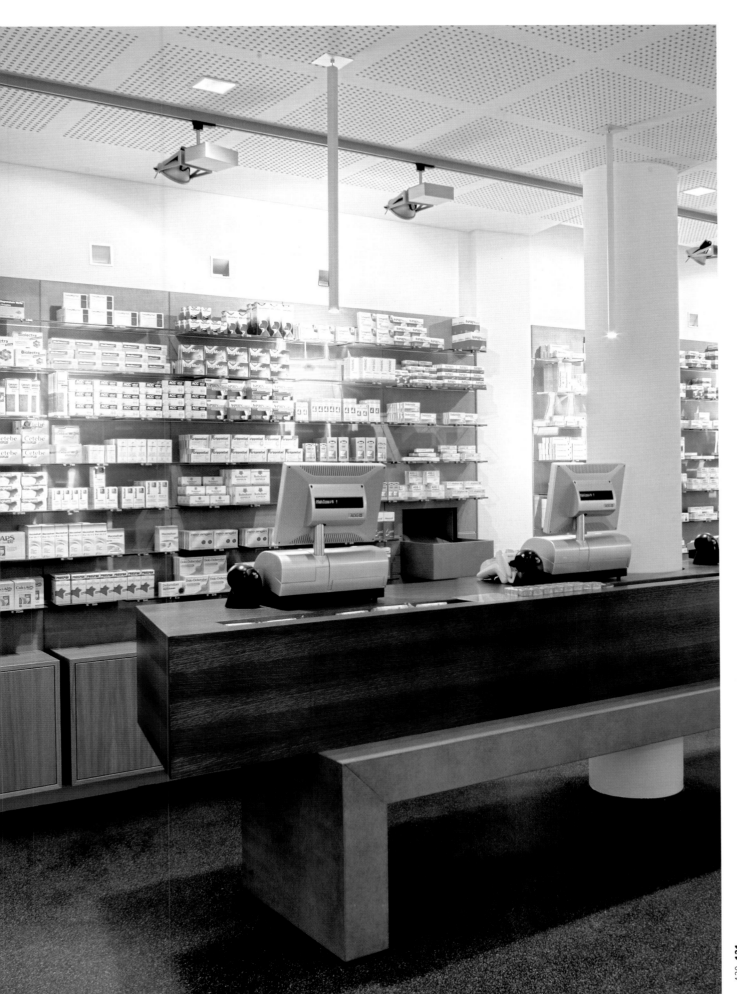

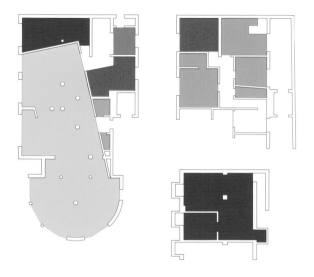

Diagrammatic plans, to scale 1:400
Floor plans, to scale 1:200

1	Sales area	**7**	Pharmaceutical assistant	**12**	Laboratory | prescription area
2	Cash desk	**8**	Stocks	**13**	Bathroom | shower
3	Self-service area	**9**	Bathroom	**14**	Night shift room | office
4	Consultations	**10**	Staff lounge | kitchen	**15**	Product storage
5	Product storage	**11**	Staff changing	**16**	Drug storage
6	Goods inwards				

GF

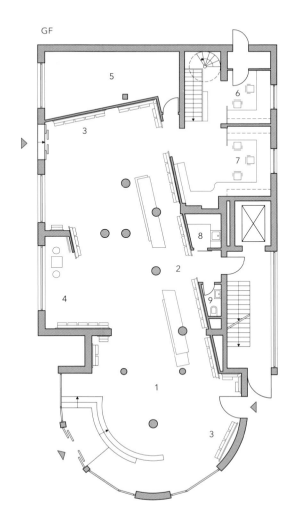

FF

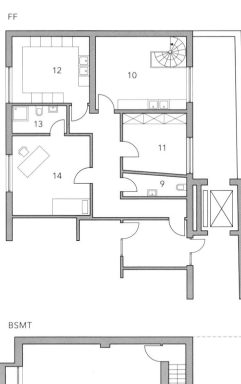

BSMT

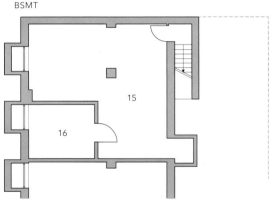

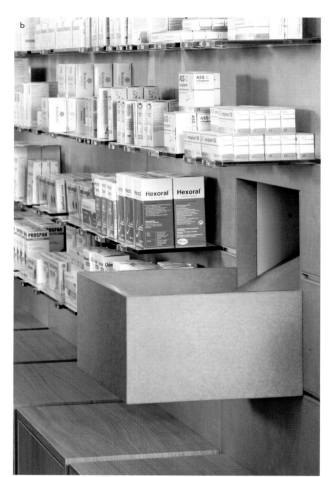

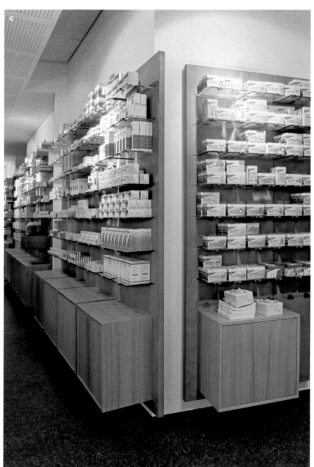

**Client	operator**	Hartmut Schnaith
Design phase	12 2005 – 03 2006
Built	08 2006 – 10 2006
Gross floor area	478 sqm
Usable surface	354 sqm
Gross volume	1,346 cbm
Construction cost	284,000 €
Total cost	340,000 €

a   The shelves at the back are used to
    screen off the private areas of the
    pharmacy.
b   Goods from the automated stockroom
    are placed on the shelves behind the till.
c   Sealed oak cubes below the shelves are
    used to store excess stock.
d   The seamless polished asphalt screed
    floor creates continuity between the old
    and new sections of the building.

Floor layout
The three-story pharmacy has adequate space, though the limited
amount of room on the first floor has required the installation of an automated stockroom. The laboratory is on the top floor. A single flight of
stairs leads to the basement stockrooms, and a spiral staircase to the
second floor.

Usable areas

Sales	**yellow**	175 sqm	49 %
Service	**red**	17 sqm	5 %
Employee areas	**orange**	62 sqm	18 %
Supply	disposal	**brown**	100 sqm	28 %
Total		354 sqm	100 %

Other key information

Catchment radius	5 km
Distance to nearest pharmacy	200 m
Nearest health facility	Medical center
Number of items in stock	8,000
Stock turnover rate	11
Proportion produced in-house	1 %
Drugs produced in-house	Salves, capsules, teas
Proportion delivered externally	10 %
Type of customers supplied	Retirement homes
Number of staff	7
Prescriptions filled per day	150
Technical facilities	Air conditioner, order picker, conveyors

Nature of special services: travel vaccination advice, seminars,
prescription delivery service

The Park-Apotheke is located on the first floor of a medical center in Potsdam. The slim building is located between two apartment blocks dating from the first half of the twentieth century, but its large windows and the fact that it juts forwards from its neighbors emphasise its public function.

Full-height display windows provide a view of the sales area, where the central focus is the large, bright green curved counter, standing in impressive contrast to the yellow-painted ceiling and dark-coloured wall-mounted shelves, which in turn hark back to traditional pharmacy interiors. The green of the counter is repeated in the staircase, where a delicate artwork extending the full height of the building contains abstract depictions of medicinal herbs. Particular attention has been paid to the lighting, with the colourful, brightly illuminated interior and large windows of the cube acting as a beacon at night.

3PO

PARK-APOTHEKE
POTSDAM | G

NEW CONSTRUCTION

PHARMACY IN HEALTHCARE
FACILITY
URBAN PHARMACY

SMALL PHARMACY

URB

SMA | PHF

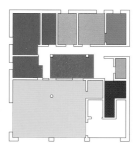

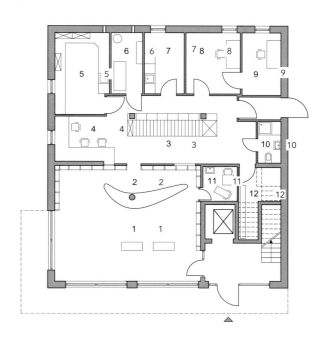

**Client	operator**	Alhorn	Kulka OHG, Ralf Alhorn, Hartmut Kulka
Design phase	01 2004 – 03 2005
Built	03 2005 – 10 2005
Usable surface	144 sqm
Construction cost	190,000 €
Total cost	240,000 €

a Dark-coloured wall-mounted shelves hark back to traditional pharmacy interiors.
b In the staircase a delicate artwork extending the full height of the building contains abstract depictions of medicinal herbs.
c The green counter takes centre stage.

Diagrammatic plans, to scale 1:400
Floor plans, to scale 1:200

Floor layout

1	Sales area		laboratory	**9**	Office
2	Cash desk	**6**	Utility room	**10**	Bathroom	shower
3	Alphabetic storage	**7**	Kitchen	**11**	Private
4	Workstation	**8**	Night shift room			consultations
5	Prescription area			office	**12**	Product storage

All operationally related rooms are well laid out.

Usable areas

Sales	**yellow**	60 sqm	42 %
Service	**red**	39 sqm	27 %
Administration	**green**	9 sqm	6 %
Employee areas	**orange**	22 sqm	15 %
Supply	disposal	**brown**	8 sqm	6 %
Plant	**blue**	6 sqm	4 %
Total		144 sqm	100 %

Other key information

Catchment radius	10 km
Distance to nearest pharmacy	200 m
Nearest health facility	Medical practice in-house Physiotherapy
Proportion produced in-house	3 %
Drugs produced in-house	Cremes, salves, solutions
Type of customers supplied	Private clients, medical practice, nursing service
Number of staff	3 – 4
Prescriptions filled per day	60
Proportion of special services	3 %

Nature of special services: advice weeks, diet counseling, homeopathy

When lit at night, the red, yellow, and green interior looks more like an upscale cocktail bar than a pharmacy. By day, the bright, colourful design catches the eyes of passers-by. The interior designer combed through 1,950 colours to select ones that produced a calming effect and an improved sense of well-being.

The store window is unusually wide at 28 metres, offering attractive views of the spacious sales area by day and night. The back walls of the three broad counters have transparent shelves and are painted to match the rest of the interior, while the individual display areas are interspersed with vertical light pillars. Likewise, the simple dark wooden counters have horizontal striplights in the same colours. The wide floorplan of the sales area has deliberately been preserved using a geometric layout of straight lines, cubes, and rectangles.

The adjoining rooms include an alphabetic storage area visible from the sales area, a sterile laboratory, and a pharmaceutical library. One innovation is the pharmacy's drive-in counter, where customers, who suffer from limited mobility or are simply in a hurry, can talk to staff via an intercom.

RENATE HAWIG

APOTHEKE IM WESTEN
BIELEFELD | G

URBAN PHARMACY

MEDIUM-SIZED
PHARMACY

URB

MED

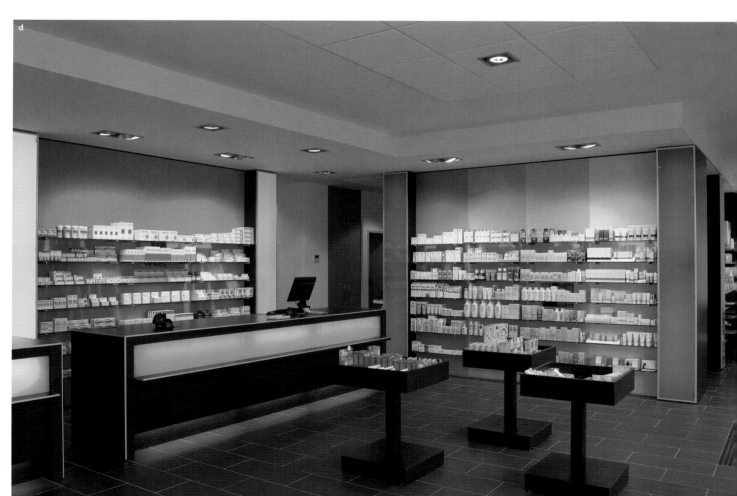

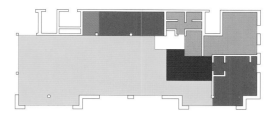

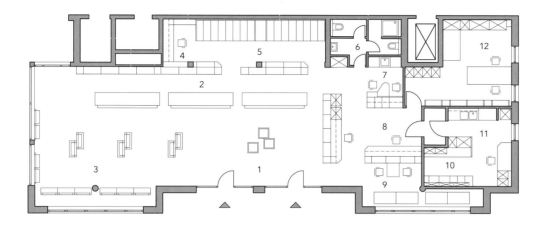

Client	operator	Bernd Schröder
Design phase	06 2006–12 2006
Built	01 2007–05 2007
Gross floor area	259 sqm
Usable surface	242 sqm
Gross volume	842 cbm
Total cost	380,000 €

a The high-tech laboratory is fitted with specialist air filters.
b The dispensary
c A laminar flow unit used to make sterile solutions.
d The space is dominated by straight lines, cubes, and rectangles.

Diagrammatic plans, to scale 1:400
Floor plans, to scale 1:200

Floor layout

1 Sales area	5 Alphabetic storage	9 Consultations
2 Cash desk	6 Bathroom	shower	10 Prescription area
3 Self-service area	7 Staff lounge	11 Laboratory
4 Office	8 Stock control	12 Night shift room

The whole pharmacy is on one floor, so distances are minimal, particularly between the customer area and alphabetic storage area. The staff rest areas are spacious, and the bathrooms conveniently located.

Usable areas

Sales	**yellow**	135 sqm	56 %
Service	**red**	47 sqm	19 %
Administration	**green**	6 sqm	2 %
Employee areas	**orange**	38 sqm	16 %
Supply	disposal	**brown**	16 sqm	7 %
Total		242 sqm	100 %

Other key information

Catchment radius	2 km
Distance to nearest pharmacy	500 m
Nearest health facility	Hospital, medical practice
Number of items in stock	9,000
Stock turnover rate	10
Proportion produced in-house	1 %
Drugs produced in-house	Solutions, salves, pills, teas
Number of staff	5 Full time
Prescriptions filled per day	100
Proportion of special services	30 %
Technical facilities	Clean air in laboratory, laminar flow machine

Nature of special services: homeopathy, biochemistry, natural medicine, GMP-compatible prescription drugs, drug searches

The tri-Haus-Apotheke, located in a health center in Arnsberg-Neheim near Dortmund, is built on a triangular site. This was a difficult project, as the interior had to be designed accordingly, and the pharmacy also needed a rear entrance in addition to the front doors in one corner of the triangle.

The sales area is only 57 square metres, but looks more spacious, with grey and beige stone floors enhancing the bright, friendly impression. The first thing visitors see is the amber-coloured rear walls, which also help to create a warm, harmonious environment, while a backlit storage unit of the same colour on the counter fosters a sense of continuity. The Wenge wood and lacquered glass furniture gives the space a strong sense of structure – an important element of the design which, given the triangular floorplan, was not easy to achieve.

The building's energy supply is highly innovative, with geothermal probes 100 metres below the ground supplying heating and air conditioning, and a 100-square-metre solar electricity array, together reducing the pharmacy's total energy consumption to that of a 32-square-metre apartment.

RENATE HAWIG

TRI-HAUS-APOTHEKE
ARNSBERG-NEHEIM | G

PHARMACY IN HEALTHCARE
FACILITY
URBAN PHARMACY

MEDIUM-SIZED
PHARMACY

URB

PHF

MED

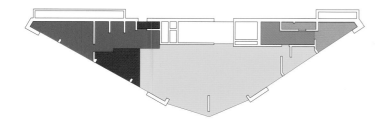

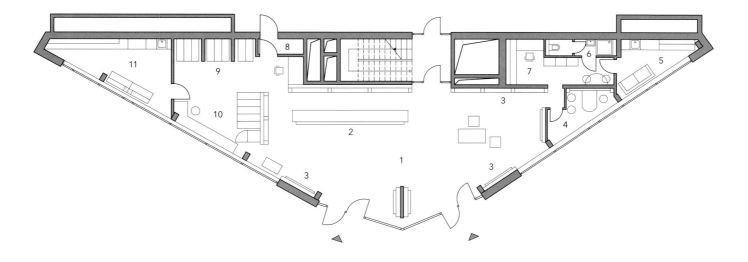

		Floor layout			
**Client	operator**	Elke Banz, Dietmar Riecks, Uwe Berbüße	**1** Sales area	**5** Night shift room	**9** Alphabetic storage
		2 Cash desk	**6** Bathroom	shower	**10** Stock control
Design phase	02 2003–11 2004	**3** Self-service area	**7** Office	**11** Prescription area	laboratory
Built	12 2004–04 2005	**4** Consultations	**8** Goods inwards	
Gross floor area	231 sqm			
Usable surface	195 sqm			
Gross volume	712 cbm			
Total cost	150,000 €			

One corner of the triangular site houses the offices and stockroom, and the other the administration and service areas. The customer area is in the middle of the building, pushing the other parts of the pharmacy out to the sides.

a Grey and beige stone floors and dark Wenge wood help to create an attractive atmosphere.

b The consulting room is behind the glowing amber-coloured self-service wall to the side of the building.

c Despite being only 57 square metres, the sales area is bright and user-friendly.

Diagrammatic plans, to scale 1:400
Floor plans, to scale 1:2000

Usable areas

Sales	**yellow**	112 sqm	57 %
Service	**red**	40 sqm	21 %
Administration	**green**	12 sqm	6 %
Employee areas	**orange**	14 sqm	7 %
Supply	disposal	**brown**	17 sqm	9 %
Total		195 sqm	100 %

Other key information

Catchment radius	4 km
Distance to nearest pharmacy	500 m
Nearest health facility	Medical practice
Number of items in stock	8,000
Stock turnover rate	6 Months
	2 Times a year
Proportion produced in-house	2 %
Drugs produced in-house	dermatology salves, uvula
Number of staff	4 Full time
Prescriptions filled per day	200
Proportion of special services	5 %
Technical facilities	Heating and cooling with geothermal probe

Nature of special services: facial diagnosis, nutritional advice, diabetic footcare

Simplicity is the watchword at the newly designed Auge-Gottes-Apotheke (Eye of God Pharmacy). The small, narrow sales area and the other rooms behind it could have been more spacious and user friendly if the basement had been an integral part of the design.

This contemporary interior has been redesigned to sell everything from humble camomile tea to state-of-the-art drugs, and is focused around the building's central axis. The pharmacy's diagonally positioned main area has been stripped of its partitioning wall and vestibule, and now opens on to the dispensary behind and to the adjoining stockroom and laboratory.

Viewed through the full-height window in the sales area, the series of back rooms appear transparent and spacious – but are screened off by the wide Zebrano wood counter. Brightly lit shelves with semicircular corners set into the wall provide ample display space. A newly built staircase leads to the wellness area in the basement, and the opposite side of the building houses a small consultation area, the second entrance to the office, and the night service area and laboratory. Outside, the yellow artificial stone façade, with its red script and big illuminated pictures of eyes, creates an unmistakable landmark at the crossing of two streets and prepares visitors for the axial interior layout.

ATELIER HEISS ARCHITEKTEN

AUGE-GOTTES-APOTHEKE
VIENNA | A

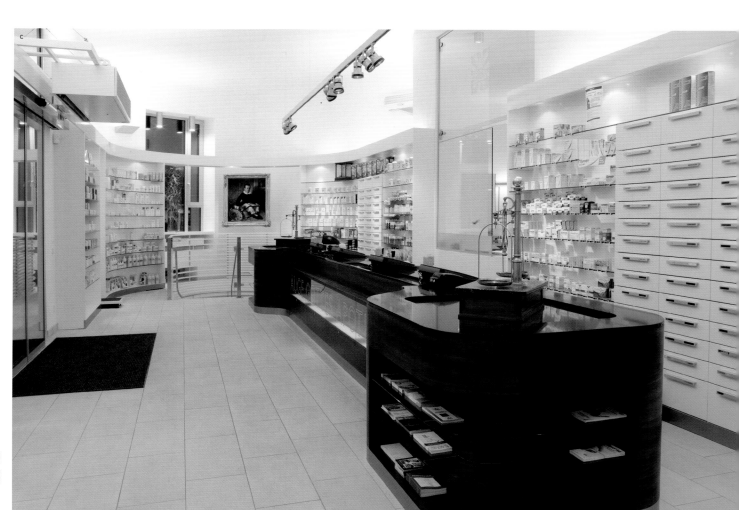

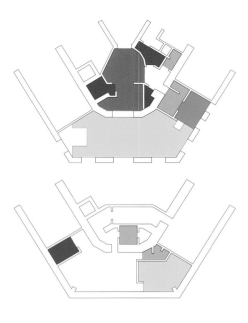

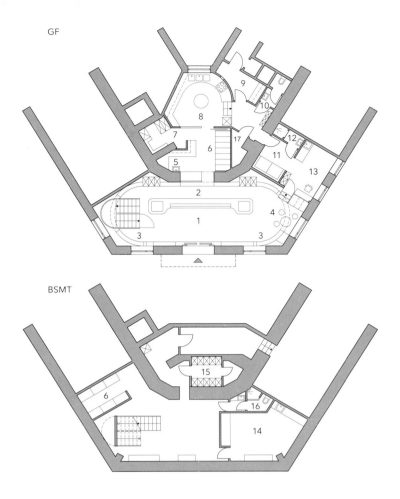

BSMT

Client | operator   Christina Kletter
Design phase   01 2005 – 08 2005
Built   08 2005 – 09 2005
Gross floor area   238 sqm
Usable surface   150 sqm

a A newly built staircase leads to the basement wellness center.
b Viewed through the full-height window in the sales area, the series of back rooms appears transparent and spacious.
c The diagonally positioned main room opens onto the dispensary behind and the adjoining stockroom and laboratory.

Diagrammatic plans, to scale 1:400
Floor plans, to scale 1:200

Floor layout

1	Sales area	**7**	Product storage	**13**	Office
2	Cash desk	**8**	Laboratory	**14**	Treatment
3	Self-service area	**9**	Goods inwards	**15**	Staff changing
4	Consultations	**10**	Bathroom	**16**	Bathroom	shower
5	Prescription area	**11**	Night shift room	**17**	Storage
6	Alphabetic storage	**12**	Shower		

Good use has been made of the existing fabric to create a user-friendly layout. However, the treatment room and wellness center in the basement have no natural light, and the extended alphabetic storage area, also in the basement, is not easily accessible.

Usable areas

Sales	**yellow**	76 sqm	51 %
Service	**red**	28 sqm	18 %
Administration	**green**	10 sqm	7 %
Employee areas	**orange**	18 sqm	12 %
Supply	disposal	**brown**	18 sqm	12 %
Total		150 sqm	100 %

Other key information

Distance to nearest pharmacy	400 m
Number of items in stock	6,000
Proportion produced in-house	3 %
Drugs produced in-house	Prescriptions
Proportion delivered externally	5 %
Type of customers supplied	Hospital
Number of staff	12
Prescriptions filled per day	300
Proportion of special services	3 %
Technical facilities	Air conditioner

Nature of special services: cosmetics, massage, blood pressure, blood sugar, and cholesterol testing

URB

SMA

This old pharmacy is located in a listed building dating from 1774 on the Freyung, a triangular public square in Vienna. It has undergone careful and effective restoration, with the emphasis on practicality and on respect for the historic fabric.

The exterior therefore remains unchanged, with the exception of a yellow glass plate in the entrance embrasure. This prepares visitors for the interior colour scheme, where the upper shelf compartments are lined with yellow glass and the shelves themselves, replaced by slightly tinted glass, make the dark shop fittings look lighter. The wallpaper was removed from the late baroque Bohemian vaulting, which was then lightly whitewashed.

The dominant yellow and the new lighting system, which makes the pharmacy particularly eyecatching at night, create a bright, cheerful atmosphere which contrasts with, but does not swamp, the seriousness and elegance of the historic interior. The original fittings are complemented by freestanding stainless steel shelves which, together with the new display cases in the center of the sales area, add a sensitive modern touch to a very traditional pharmacy.

ATELIER HEISS ARCHITEKTEN

APOTHEKE "ZU UNSERER LIEBEN FRAU BEI DEN SCHOTTEN"
VIENNA | A

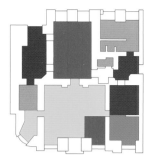

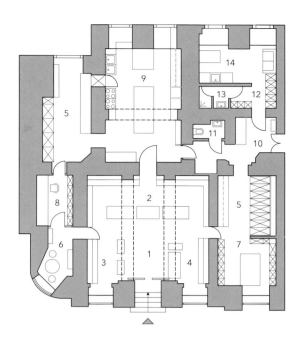

Client | operator Stephan Höbinger
Design phase 12 2002–07 2003
Built 07 2003–08 2003
Gross floor area 180 sqm
Usable surface 149 sqm

a The new display cases in the center of the sales area add a sensitive modern touch to a very traditional pharmacy.
b The interior is decorated with historic glass and porcelain containers.
c The old pharmacy scales remain in their traditional position on the counter.
d The wallpaper was removed from the late baroque Bohemian vaulting, which was then whitewashed.

Diagrammatic plans, to scale 1:400
Floor plans, to scale 1:200

Floor layout

1 Sales area	**6** Consultations	**11** Bathroom
2 Cash desk	**7** Office	**12** Staff changing
3 Self-service area	**8** Workstation	**13** Shower
4 Prescription area	**9** Laboratory	**14** Night shift room
5 Product storage	**10** Goods inwards	

The existing building was highly suitable for use as a pharmacy. Unfortunately, there is no daylight in the workroom, and the positions of the staff rest area and stockroom could have been reversed to place the laboratory closer to the goods inwards area.

Usable areas

Sales	**yellow**	45 sqm	30 %
Service	**red**	35 sqm	23 %
Administration	**green**	11 sqm	8 %
Employee areas	**orange**	23 sqm	15 %
Supply | disposal	**brown**	35 sqm	24 %
Total		149 sqm	100 %

Other key information

Catchment radius	0,3 km
Distance to nearest pharmacy	200 m
Number of items in stock	6,000
Proportion produced in-house	10 %
Drugs produced in-house	TCM, salves
Proportion delivered externally	2 %
Type of customers supplied	Private clients
Number of staff	4 Full time, 8 Part time
Prescriptions filled per day	70
Nature of special services	TCM

Many hurdles had to be overcome in building the St. Anna Apotheke [1828] in central Munich, making the interior design even more spectacular. The small site, only just large enough to reach the minimum legal size for a pharmacy, extends over two floors. The owner's desire for a modern, individual design had to be reconciled with the need to protect the listed building.

The interior is dominated by ceiling-height, wall-mounted shelves painted in signal-red car paint that separate the customer area from the dispensary. There is no window display, so the shelves are the first things to catch the visitor's eye, and the only external signage is an inscription on a pillar and the green-cross international pharmacy symbol in the windows. The wall-mounted shelves extend into the rear half of the interior, making space for the simple, white-painted counter.

Behind this are the workroom, dispensary, and stairs to the upper floor, which houses a stockroom only seven square metres in area. This contains a fully automatic stock picker connected to the sales area by a transportation system in the timber-beamed ceiling. A small office was constructed for the pharmacist in what was previously a storage room; the specially made green glass wall and lifting device are the most instantly noticeable feature of the staircase.

HUBER RÖSSLER ARCHITEKTUR-BÜRO

ST. ANNA APOTHEKE [1828]
MUNICH | G

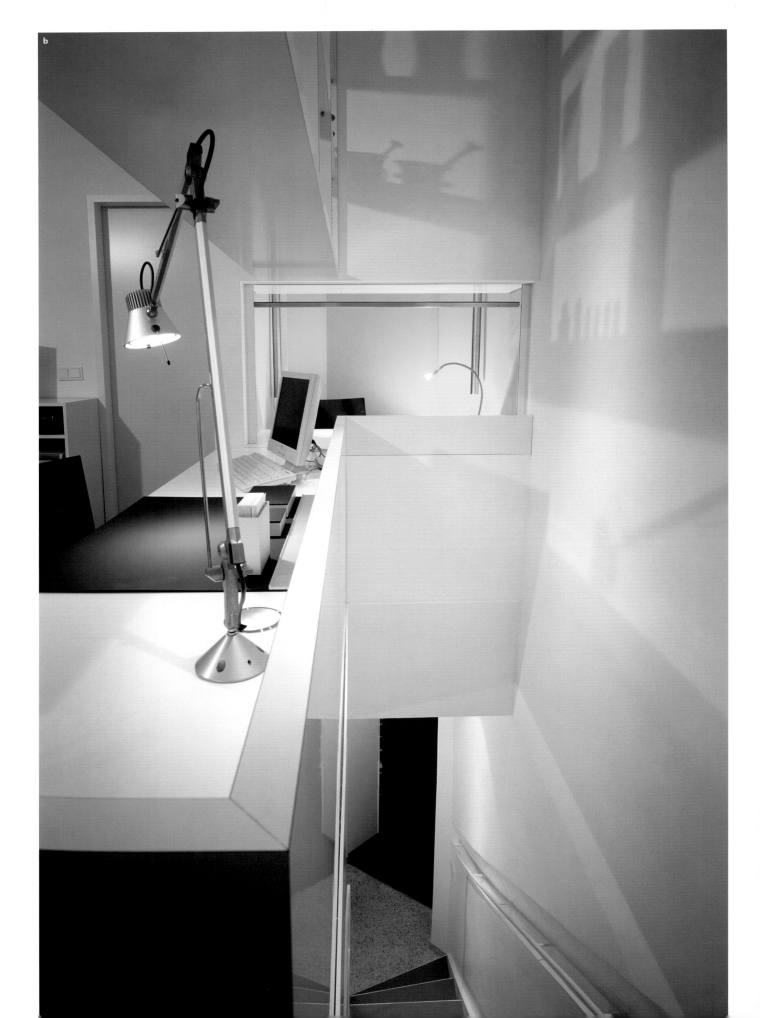

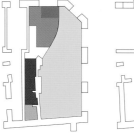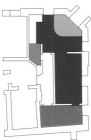

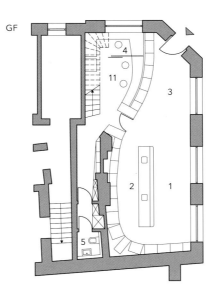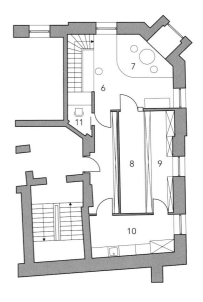

Client | operator	Ludwig Gierstorfer jr.
Design phase	11 2002–02 2003
Built	02 2003–04 2003
Usable surface	124 sqm
Gross volume	604 cbm

a The interior is dominated by a full-height, wall-mounted shelf unit painted in signal red car paint.

b The pharmacist's lemon yellow mini-office on the upper floor

c The counterweight of the sash window in the office

d A deliberate decision was made not to incorporate a window display, and instead the wall of red shelves has been used to attract passers-by.

e The workroom and dispensary are visible from outside.

Diagrammatic plans, to scale 1:400
Floor plans, to scale 1:200

Floor layout

1	Sales area	**5**	Bathroom	**9**	Product storage
2	Cash desk	**6**	Stock control	**10**	Laboratory
3	Self-service area	**7**	Night shift room	**11**	Office
4	Prescription area	**8**	Product storage		

Because the pharmacy is located in a two-story historic building, it is not always very practically laid out. It is not easy to carry products from the first floor up the angular staircase to the second-floor stockrooms, or to access the laboratory and workstations.

Usable areas

Sales	**yellow**	49 sqm	40 %
Service	**red**	14 sqm	12 %
Administration	**green**	13 sqm	10 %
Employee areas	**orange**	9 sqm	7 %
Supply | disposal	**brown**	39 sqm	31 %
Total		124 sqm	100 %

Other key information

Distance to nearest pharmacy	300 m
Nearest health facility	Medical practice
Number of items in stock	20,000
Proportion produced in-house	5 %
Drugs produced in-house	Salves, capsules, teas, uvula
Proportion delivered externally	15 %
Type of customers supplied	Medical practice, retirement homes, clinics, private clients
Number of staff	8 Full time, 5 Part time [+ messengers]
Technical facilities	Product storage, order picker

Nature of special services: skin cosmetics, oncology, inhouse production, prescription development, searches

The granite floor of the Linden Apotheke draws on the baroque architecture of Ludwigsburg. Full-length white shelves, some of them set into the wall, and rooms with rounded corners make the sales area look compact, with carefully designed lighting creating a strong background for the goods on display.

The main focus is on the white counter jutting out on either side of the ceiling supports. Three revolving displays are used for seasonal products and their white circular bases making them stand out from the otherwise uniform cobble flooring.

However, the interior's most distinctive feature is the ornamental ceiling. The strong, bold lines and pale monochrome furnishings lead the eye to the colourful fresco depicting eleven medicinal herbs in a modern interpretation of a traditional colour scheme. The pharmacist specialises in natural medicine and cosmetics, and the whole corporate design was changed to reflect this. The emphasis on herbs, the old-fashioned floor covering and the dominance of the fresco express pharmaceutical traditions in a simple form.

IPPOLITO FLEITZ GROUP

LINDEN APOTHEKE
LUDWIGSBURG | G

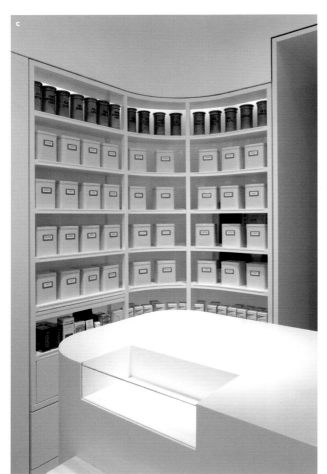

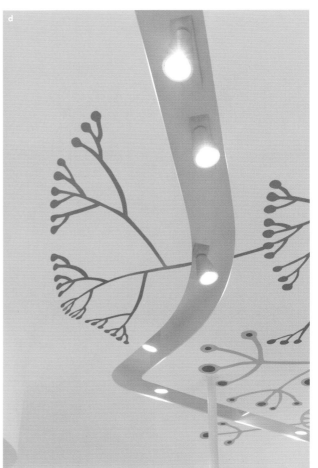

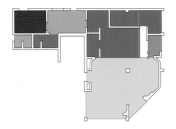

Client | operator	Meike Raasch	
Design phase	12 2005 – 06 2006	
Built	05 2006 – 06 2006	
Usable surface	120 sqm	
Gross volume	361 cbm	

a The granite-cobbled floor is a reference to Ludwigsburg's baroque architecture.

b The white counter extends outwards on both sides of the ceiling support.

c White shelves set into the wall and rooms with round corners make the sales area look compact.

d The colourful plant motifs of the ceiling fresco are a modern take on a traditional theme.

e Three revolving display stands are used for seasonal products.

Diagrammatic plans, to scale 1:400
Floor plans, to scale 1:200

Floor layout

1 Sales area	**5** Office	**9** Night shift room
2 Cash desk	**6** Prescription area	**10** Product storage
3 Self-service area	**7** Laboratory	**11** Plant room
4 Alphabetic storage	**8** Workstation	**12** Bathroom

Every inch of the limited space available in this one-story pharmacy has been put to good use. However, the stockroom is reached via the night service area, and the bathroom is not as accessible as it could be.

Usable areas

Sales	**yellow**	50 sqm	42 %
Service	**red**	37 sqm	31 %
Administration	**green**	4 sqm	3 %
Employee areas	**orange**	15 sqm	13 %
Supply | disposal	**brown**	10 sqm	8 %
Plant	**blue**	4 sqm	3 %
Total		120 sqm	100 %

Other key information

Catchment radius	15 km
Distance to nearest pharmacy	350 m
Nearest health facility	Medical practice, medical houses
Number of items in stock	8,000
Stock turnover rate	2,5
Proportion produced in-house	5 %
Drugs produced in-house	Salves, juices, uvula, teas, eyedrops
Type of customers supplied	Regular and walk-in customers
Number of staff	3
Technical facilities	Air conditioner

Multipurpose counters run almost the full length of the Adler-Apotheke's large sales area, which has entrances at both ends and forms the main axis of the pharmacy. It ends with a glass dispensary extending the small laboratory into the sales area. When the pharmacy was redesigned, the size differential between the large sales area and compact storages and work area was changed, and the spacious self-service section became a feature in its own right.

The main colour is white, but splashes of bright green lighten the wide room and contrast with the pale-coloured shelving and the grainy Zebrano wood of the long counter. Referred to by the architects as the command center, this is divided into several areas which resolve themselves into smaller consultation and sales counters towards the main entrance.

Self-service items are arranged by size in so-called "para-sites" on the counter and in freestanding wheeled satellite display units dispersed around the sales area. Full-length shelves have been fitted behind the counter and in the empty spaces between the ceiling-height windows to the street. There is no window display, and instead the design relies on the effect of the colourful pharmaceutical products, which make the sales area itself look like a carefully arranged shop window. At the back of the pharmacy, hidden behind the glass-walled dispensary, are workstations, a laboratory, and an office.

KINZO

ADLER-APOTHEKE
BERLIN | G

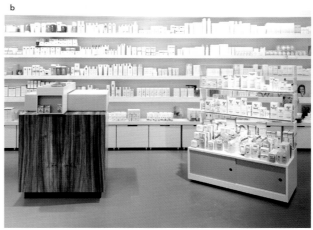

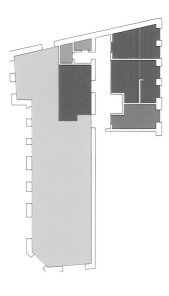

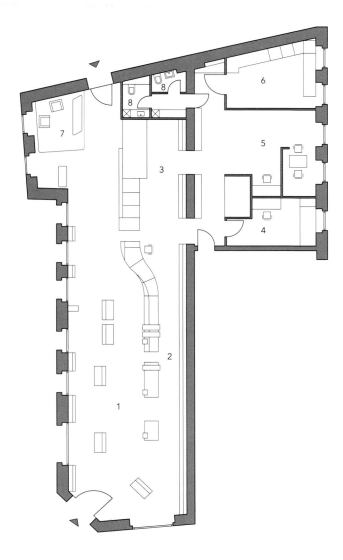

**Client	operator**	Azim Zia
Design phase	01 2003 – 08 2003
Built	08 2003 – 11 2003
Gross floor area	280 sqm
Usable surface	232 sqm
Construction cost	110,000 €
Total cost	180,000 €

a The main colour is white, but splashes of brilliant green brighten the wide room.
b Additional self-service items are displayed in mobile satellite units around the room.
c The grainy Zebrano wood counter contrasts with the pale-coloured shelves behind the counter.
d The long counter is the dominant feature of the sales area, and ends at the glass-partitioned dispensary.

Diagrammatic plans, to scale 1:400
Floor plans, to scale 1:200

Floor layout

1	Sales area	**4**	Office	**7**	Treatment
2	Cash desk	**5**	Workstation	**8**	Bathroom
3	Prescription area	**6**	Laboratory		

The distances between key areas of the pharmacy are short, particularly between the customer area and dispensary. The supply and waste disposal areas are not shown.

Usable areas

Sales	**yellow**	148 sqm	64 %
Service	**red**	65 sqm	28 %
Administration	**green**	14 sqm	6 %
Employee areas	**orange**	5 sqm	2 %
Total		232 sqm	100 %

Other key information

Catchment radius	5 km
Distance to nearest pharmacy	40 m
Nearest health facility	none
Number of items in stock	5,000
Stock turnover rate	13
Proportion produced in-house	2 %
Drugs produced in-house	Salves
Proportion delivered externally	10 %
Type of customers supplied	Regular and walk-in customers
Number of staff	5
Prescriptions filled per day	170
Proportion of special services	5 %
Technical facilities	Air conditioner

Nature of special services: cosmetic treatments, blood pressure, blood sugar, and cholesterol testing, travel medicine advice

The Paulus Apotheke was extensively expanded and refurbished in 2001, with the cramped layout being replaced by an open-plan design in bright, friendly colours. In 2006, the pharmacist decided to set up a consultation room in an additional rented area to provide clients with a wider range of products and services.

In the Red Lounge, she offers facial analysis, Bach flower remedies, and cosmetic advice. This also serves as a rest area for staff, a venue for confidential individual health advice sessions, and an additional back office. To fit all these functions into a space only 35 square metres in area, the architect produced a multipurpose design.

Full-height white fitted furniture with integrated storage divides the lounge into islands framed by a "panoramic shelf": A bright red eye-level niche that combines all of these functions, echoing the red of the lino and contrasting sharply with the simple white fitted closets. To respond flexibly to a variety of needs, some of the areas can be partitioned off using full-height curtains on curving rails fitted to the ceiling.

THOMAS MAIERHOFER

EXPANSION OF PAULUS APOTHEKE "RED LOUNGE"
VIENNA | A

EXPANSION

URBAN PHARMACY

MEDIUM-SIZED
PHARMACY

URB

MED

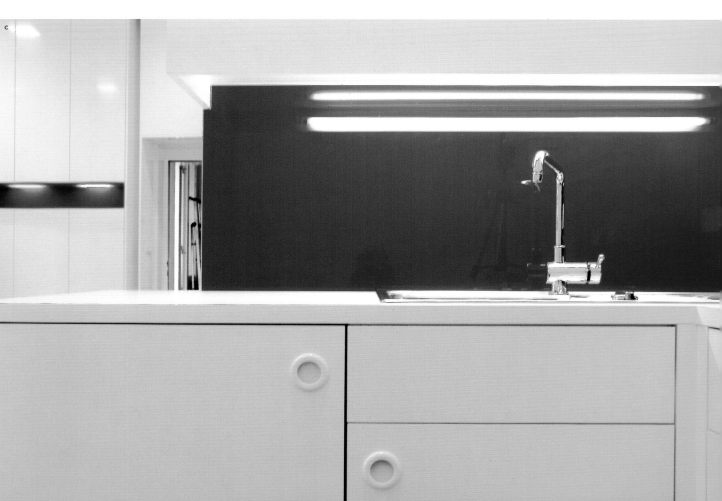

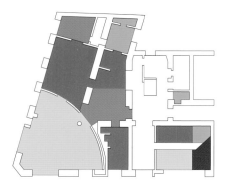

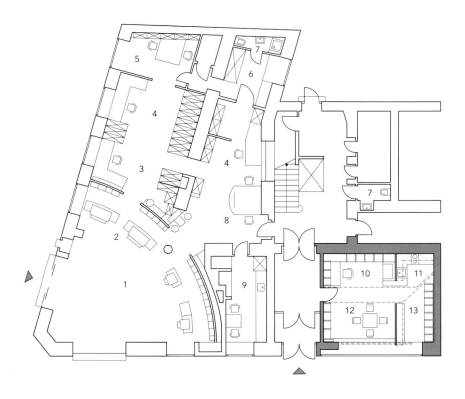

Client	operator	Christa Wenkoff
Design phase	05 2006–10 2006
Built	10 2006–11 2006
Usable surface	201 sqm

a The "panoramic shelf", a bright red eye-level niche, brings together all the various areas of the addition.

b Full-height white fitted furniture with integrated storage space divides the lounge into islands.

c Bright red and gleaming white make for a stark contrast.

Diagrammatic plans, to scale 1:400
Floor plans, to scale 1:200

Floor layout

1	Sales area	**6**	Shift room	**11**	Kitchen
2	Cash desk	**7**	Bathroom	**12**	Consultations
3	Prescription area	**8**	Orders	**13**	Product storage
4	Alphabetic storage	**9**	Laboratory		
5	Office	**10**	Workstation		

The existing pharmacy was expanded by renting extra space. An unusual solution is the shared use of the separately accessible room [nos 10- 13] which is divided into four different areas for customer advice and operational purposes.

Usable areas

Sales	**yellow**	75 sqm	37 %
Service	**red**	70 sqm	35 %
Administration	**green**	31 sqm	15 %
Employee areas	**orange**	18 sqm	9 %
Supply | disposal	**brown**	7 sqm	4 %
Total		201 sqm	100 %

Other key information

Catchment radius	0,5 km
Distance to nearest pharmacy	500 m
Number of items in stock	8,000
Stock turnover rate	13
Proportion produced in-house	2 %
Drugs produced in-house	Salves, teas, uvula, capsules
Proportion delivered externally	10 %
Type of customers supplied	Retirement homes
Number of staff	15
Prescriptions filled per day	200
Proportion of special services	10 %
Technical facilities	Air conditioner, laminar air flow

Nature of special services: bach flower remedies, homeopathic advice, and in-house production, facial and skin analysis, smoking cessation, vascular testing, screening program

The new central pharmacy at Frankenthal municipal hospital also supplies six other hospitals in Rhineland-Palatinate and Baden-Wuerttemberg, with a total of 1,500 beds. Not all hospitals maintain their own pharmacies; increasing numbers now pool their resources with others.

The pharmaceutical and medical products service center is on the first floor of the Frankenthal hospital, a solid 1970s building. Goods can be brought in and out without an elevator, and the hospital's delivery area can also be used.

The pharmacy uses a semi-automated stock picker to save space, which staff have found to be more laboratory-intensive but also more efficient than a fully automatic one. Particular attention has been given to making the pharmacy an attractive workplace, with its contemporary lighting and colour scheme and bright, friendly materials.

SANDER HOFRICHTER

APOTHEKE STADTKLINIK
FRANKENTHAL | G

PHARMACY IN HEALTHCARE
FACILITY
URBAN PHARMACY

LARGE PHARMACY

REDESIGN

URB

PHF

LAR

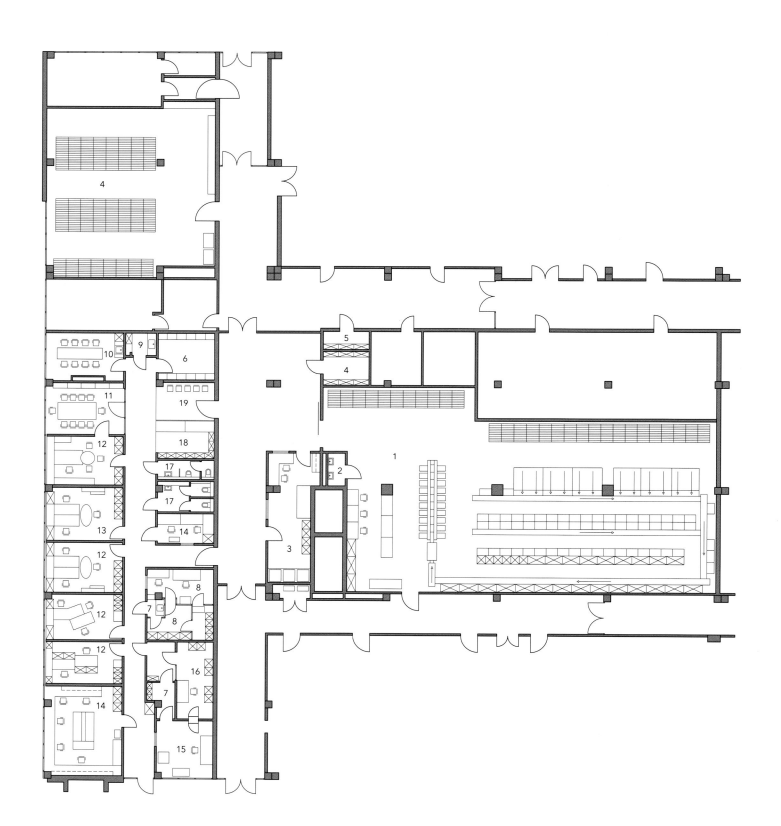

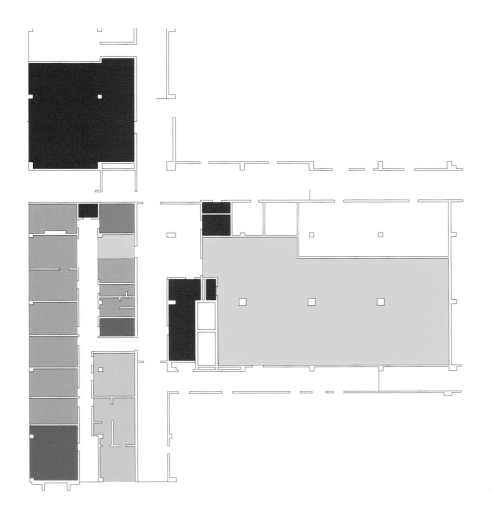

Diagrammatic plans, to scale 1:400
Floor plans, to scale 1:200

1	Sales area	**7**	Sluice	**13**	Orders
2	Cleaning equipment	**8**	Parenterals	**14**	Laboratory
	storage	**9**	Disposal	**15**	Cytostatics
3	Goods inwards	**10**	Staff lounge	**16**	Preparation room
4	Drug storage	**11**	Meeting area |	**17**	Bathroom
5	Emergency storage		library	**18**	Staff sales
6	Archive	**12**	Shift room	**19**	Reception

Client | operator	Stadt Frankenthal		
Design phase	07 2004 – 04 2005		
Built	05 2005 – 04 2006		
Gross floor area	1,300 sqm		
Usable surface	827 sqm		
Gross volume	5,148 cbm		
Construction cost	950,000 €		
Total cost	1,200,000 €		

a The cleanroom is used to make parenterals.
b The rooms feature contemporary colours and lighting and bright, friendly materials.
c The corridor to the consultation room
d The pharmacy's semi-automated stock picker

Floor layout

The pharmaceutical and medical products service center consists of two areas which are separated by a wide aisle: the pharmacy itself, with a semi-automated stock picker, the adjoining goods inwards, and administration areas.

Usable areas

Sales	**yellow**	11 sqm	1 %
Service	**red**	398 sqm	48 %
Specialist areas	**pink**	64 sqm	8 %
Administration	**green**	8 sqm	1 %
Employee areas	**orange**	156 sqm	19 %
Supply | disposal	**brown**	190 sqm	23 %
Total		827 sqm	100 %

Other key information

Catchment radius	50 km
Number of items in stock	2,300
Stock turnover rate	4 – 5
Proportion produced in-house	20 %
Drugs produced in-house	Sterile drugs
Proportion delivered externally	80 %
Type of customers supplied	Hospital
Number of staff	9 Full time, 11 Part time
Proportion of special services	20 %
Technical facilities	Order picker, sterile laboratory, air conditioner
Nature of special services	Sterile production

Bright yellow is the recurring theme of the redesigned humanitas 21 pharmacy in Vienna. The architects needed to add light and transparency to an otherwise dark interior, since the building was listed and the exterior could not be significantly altered.

In the absence of any partitioning walls, the new rectangular interior is bathed in warm light almost like direct sunlight. The pillars, counter, and floor covering are all primarily yellow, and the linearity of the space is emphasised by horizontal yellow stripes. The horizontal structure above the façade acts as a semi-transparent filter, creating strong contrasts of light and shade. The pixel-raster cloud motif is repeated inside the pharmacy on the twenty-metre-long transmitted light plane on the wall behind the counters.

An organically shaped floor pattern leads customers into the pharmacy, with the small, staggered counters set slightly obliquely to the entrance to make them more inviting, and the fluorescent tube lighting also serving as guidance. The design is simple but elegant: glass, matt-painted Eternit, epoxy resin, grey, and a huge amount of yellow.

STADTGUT

HUMANITAS 21
VIENNA | A

Diagrammatic plans, to scale 1:400
Floor plans, to scale 1:200

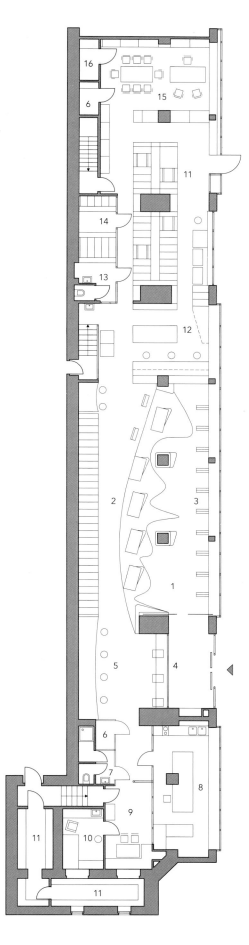

1 Sales area
2 Cash desk
3 Self-service area
4 Night dispensing area
5 Prescription area
6 Storage
7 Bathroom | shower
8 Laboratory
9 Staff lounge
10 Night shift room
11 Product storage
12 Stock control
13 Bathroom
14 Staff changing
15 Office | meeting area
16 Server room

Client | operator	Martin Mähr
Design phase	11 2002–04 2003
Built	05 2003–09 2003
Gross floor area	466 sqm
Usable surface	369 sqm
Gross volume	2,340 cbm
Construction cost	398,000 €
Total cost	456,000 €

a The yellow, organic floor patterning gives the room a graceful, flowing feel.

b The horizontal grid above the façade, which is transparent or translucent depending on the angle from which it is viewed, creates an effective interplay of light and shade inside the pharmacy.

c The night service area is simple and functional.

d The glass cladding, with fluorescent strip lighting behind it, makes the pillars in the center of the room look much more graceful.

Floor layout

The highly elongated floor plan means that the rooms have to be set one beside the other, which requires a considerable amount of walking. The rooms are arranged to the left and right of the pharmacy: storages and staff lounges are on both sides, and anyone going from one to the other has to pass through the customer area.

Usable areas

Sales	**yellow**	126 sqm	34 %
Service	**red**	59 sqm	16 %
Administration	**green**	28 sqm	8 %
Employee areas	**orange**	40 sqm	11 %
Supply | disposal	**brown**	116 sqm	31 %
Total		369 sqm	100 %

Other key information

Catchment radius	0,5 km
Distance to nearest pharmacy	700 m
Nearest health facility	Medical practice
Number of items in stock	6,500
Stock turnover rate	14
Proportion produced in-house	under 3 %
Drugs produced in-house	Salves, capsules, teas
Type of customers supplied	Regular and walk-in customers
Number of staff	19
Technical facilities	Air conditioner

The historic Einhorn-Apotheke in Linz has been family-owned for over 100 years. In preparation for handing over the business to the next generation, the pharmacy has been modified and a customer- and wheelchair-friendly entrance added.

The existing storefront was replaced by a full-height post-and-beam construction, and the central entrance moved to the side, making the bright, welcoming sales area more visible from the outside and leading the eye straight to the simple counters. The large self-service area created by the reconstruction offers ample display space in the form of closely-spaced shelves along the walls, while vertical mat plexiglass screens separate the individual product groups.

The interior uses only two colours. All horizontal surfaces, including the shelves, worktops and Bitu-Terrazzo flooring, are black, while all vertical surfaces are white Eternit Ivory. Less is more, and the restricted choice of materials and restrained fittings offer a modern, minimalist setting for a traditional family business.

PIA UND MATTHIAS LANGMAYR TP3 ARCHITEKTEN FRANZ MOSER

EINHORN-APOTHEKE
LINZ | A

REDESIGN

URBAN PHARMACY

MEDIUM-SIZED
PHARMACY

URB

MED

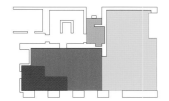

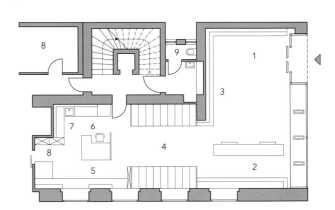

Client | operator	Katharina Mohr
Design phase	01 2006 – 08 2006
Built	09 2006 – 04 2007
Gross floor area	119 sqm
Usable surface	113 sqm
Gross volume	392 cbm

a The linear counters are the first thing customers see as they enter.
b The limited choice of materials offers a minimalist setting for the pharmacy's wares.
c All horizontal surfaces, including the floor, are black; all vertical surfaces are white.

Diagrammatic plans, to scale 1:400
Floor plans, to scale 1:200

Floor layout

1 Sales area	**4** Alphabetic storage	**7** Prescription area
2 Cash desk	**5** Stock control	**8** Product storage
3 Self-service area	**6** Workstation	**9** Bathroom

The pharmacy is laid out with the emphasis on convenience. The upper floor, which is not shown here, houses the night service area, staff lounge, laboratory, and additional storage.

Usable areas

Sales	**yellow**	55 sqm	49 %
Service	**red**	31 sqm	27 %
Employee areas	**orange**	6 sqm	5 %
Supply | disposal	**brown**	21 sqm	19 %
Total		113 sqm	100 %

Other key information

Distance to nearest pharmacy	500 m
Nearest health facility	Medical practice
Number of items in stock	5,000 – 6,000
Drugs produced in-house	Cremes, teas, juices
Number of staff	12
Prescriptions filled per day	200 – 300
Technical facilities	Air conditioner, laminar flow machine

Nature of special services: travel medicine, dietary advice, fitness coaching, homeopathy, cosmetics, allergy advice, diabetes counseling

The "Zu Maria Trost" pharmacy and its attached drugstore, located in an old market building in Kirchberg, has undergone extensive redesign. The drugstore was vacated and the whole interior layout reorganised.

Visitors now enter a spacious sales area, made more inviting by the incorporation into the new building of the lintel created when the wall was broken through. This creates an open-plan space, with the windows being widened and deepened to admit more light and restore the building's original external appearance.

The materials used for the interior fittings are white Parapan and blue Corian which, in combination with backlit blue plexiglass, create an extremely attractive space. The pharmacy's simple forms and limited choice of materials and colours make it perfect for a logically structured display.

TP3 ARCHITEKTEN FRANZ MOSER

APOTHEKE "ZU MARIA TROST"
KIRCHBERG AM WAGRAM | A

VITAMINE

PHARMACY WITHIN
DEPARTMENT STORE
RURAL PHARMACY

MEDIUM-SIZED
PHARMACY

MFD   DEP   RUR

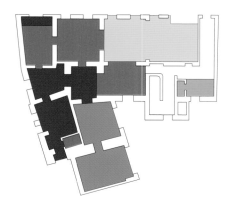

Client | operator   Ernst Becker
Design phase   04 2005 – 08 2006
Built   05 2006 – 09 2006
Gross floor area   295 sqm
Usable surface   219 sqm
Gross volume   910 cbm

a The new built-in shelves are incorporated into the lintel created when the wall was broken through.
b The dispensary adjoining the pharmacy
c The limited selection of materials and colours makes the pharmacy a perfect display setting.

Diagrammatic plans, to scale 1:400
Floor plans, to scale 1:200

Floor layout

1 Sales area	**7** Prescription pick-up	trade literature	**12** Drug storage
2 Cash desk	**8** Workstation	**13** Alphabetic storage
3 Self-service area	**9** Goods inwards	**14** Office
4 Night dispensing area	**10** Laboratory	**15** Server room
5 Consultations	**11** Product storage	**16** Bathroom
6 Prescription area		**17** Staff changing

The redesign has created a series of conveniently arranged spaces, though goods have to be carried through the laboratory, and the staff changing room and bathroom are on the outside of the building. The night service area and lounge are on the second floor, which is not shown.

Usable areas

Sales	**yellow**	53 sqm	24 %
Service	**red**	64 sqm	29 %
Administration	**green**	44 sqm	20 %
Employee areas	**orange**	8 sqm	4 %
Supply	disposal	**brown**	50 sqm	23 %
Total		219 sqm	100 %

Other key information

Catchment radius	10 km
Distance to nearest pharmacy	11 km
Nearest health facility	Medical practice
Number of items in stock	4,000
Stock turnover rate	10–12
Proportion produced in-house	5 %
Drugs produced in-house	Salves, teas
Proportion delivered externally	0 %
Type of customers supplied	Walk-in customers
Number of staff	6
Prescriptions filled per day	300
Proportion of special services	2 %
Technical facilities	Air conditioner

Nature of special services: blood pressure, blood sugar, and cholesterol testing

The distinctive bright red cube advertises the new Atrium Apotheke's presence from afar. This relatively small store is located on the main street leading into the town and is having to compete with shopping malls and much bigger rivals. It has two courtyards: one, the fully glazed first-floor atrium after which it is named, and the other a terrace on the second floor. The roofed entrance area is also a section cut out of the cube.

Different materials have been used for the various parts of the back of the building; the storage and laboratory is a black box facing onto the street, while the sheet metal and timber customer area faces towards the back of the building, which is quieter. The cubes in and above the red main section are equally striking whether viewed from the inside or outside, particularly given the astute use of downlighting.

The bright, airy interior of the pharmacy uses dark red as its focal point, with shelves suspended from the ceiling increasing this sense of openness and also serving as transparent partitions between the entrance and the three-part counter.

FLORIAN BRAND
HANNES HUEMER
TP3 ARCHITEKTEN

ATRIUM APOTHEKE
SCHWANENSTADT | A

a

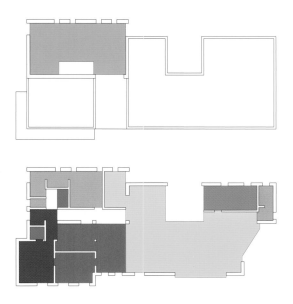

Diagrammatic plans, to scale 1:400
Floor plans, to scale 1:200

1	Sales area	**7**	Product storage	**13**	Night shift room
2	Cash desk	**8**	Alphabetic storage	**14**	Cosmetics
3	Bathroom	**9**	Plant room	**15**	Night shift desk | drive-in
4	Office	**10**	Goods inwards		
5	Prescription area	**11**	Staff changing	**16**	Multipurpose room
6	Laboratory	**12**	Shower		

TP

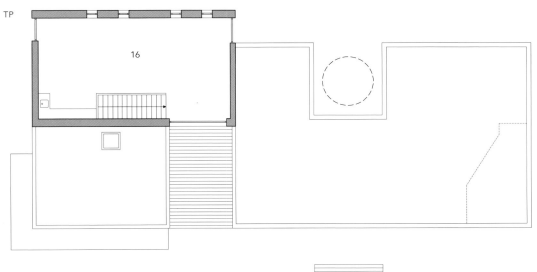

GF

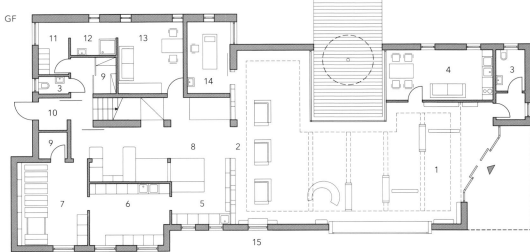

URB

LAR

**Client	operator**	Doris Leitner-Gratzei
Design phase	2006
Built	2007
Gross floor area	444 sqm
Usable surface	317 sqm
Gross volume	1,610 cbm
Construction cost	553,000 €
Total cost	782,000 €

a The vivid red of the cube is echoed inside the building.
b Shelves hanging from the ceiling enhance the sense of openness.
c Customers have to walk the full length of the sales area to reach the three-part counter.
d The interior of the pharmacy is very bright and airy.

Floor layout
Most of the pharmacy is well laid out, though the office has no direct access to the operating and storage areas. One plus point is the easy accessibility of the customer bathroom.

Usable areas

Sales	**yellow**	122 sqm	38 %
Service	**red**	49 sqm	15 %
Administration	**green**	17 sqm	5 %
Employee areas	**orange**	38 sqm	12 %
Supply	disposal	**brown**	27 sqm	9 %
Training	**violet**	59 sqm	19 %
Plant	**blue**	5 sqm	2 %
Total		317 sqm	100 %

Other key information

Catchment radius	4 km
Distance to nearest pharmacy	500 m
Number of items in stock	5,500
Drugs produced in-house	Homoeopathy
Type of customers supplied	Retirement home
Number of staff	2 Full time, 7 Part time
Prescriptions filled per day	150
Technical facilities	Air conditioner, heat pump

Nature of special services: cosmetic treatment, homeopathy, preventive health, face analysis

solarCity is a new, sustainable residential district of Linz. The highly geometric design of this city within a city is reflected in the pharmacy of the same name, whose interior is designed to match its futuristic surroundings.

The pharmacy's structure is one of strict geometric forms and lines. It occupies the whole first floor of a largely glass building and has the traditional floorplan of a pharmacy, divided equally between a customer area and a private section at the rear, with a wide wooden counter separating the two. The colours of the simple glass shelves, whose backs are painted, echo the gleaming rainbow-coloured glass roof above the square outside the pharmacy.

The full-height, horizontally divided windows make the whole of the interior visible from outside, acting as an advertisement for itself. The horizontal structure of the façade, with its bands of windows and wooden panels, is continued inside with the horizontal wall-mounted shelves and counter, whose surface-grained Zebrano wood veneer is reminiscent of the wooden paneled façade.

THILO WOLF

APOTHEKE "SOLARCITY"
LINZ | A

NEW CONSTRUCTION

URBAN PHARMACY

MEDIUM-SIZED
PHARMACY

URB

MED

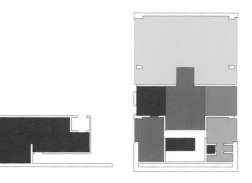

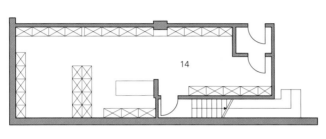

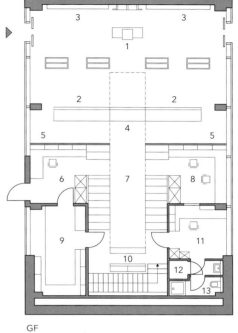

BSMT

GF

Client | operator Dietburg
                      Wilflingseder
Usable surface   242 sqm
Construction cost 300,000 €
Total cost   450,000 €

a The whole of the sales area is visible
   from outside through the full-height,
   horizontally divided windows
b The alphabetic storage area at the back
   of the pharmacy
c The specialist storage area, with steps at
   the back leading down to the basement
   storage
d The pharmacy's structure is one of strict
   geometric forms and lines.

Diagrammatic plans, to scale 1:400
Floor plans, to scale 1:200

Floor layout

1	Sales area		shelves	**10**	Drug storage
2	Cash desk	**6**	Goods inwards	**11**	Night shift room
3	Self-service area	**7**	Alphabetic storage	**12**	Storage
4	Prescription area	**8**	Orders	**13**	Bathroom	shower
5	Behind-the-counter	**9**	Laboratory	**14**	Product storage

The near-symmetrical floorplan means that the interior is well laid out,
with operations areas and storages on one side, offices and service areas
on the other, and the dispensary in the middle. The basement storage
area is easily accessible, but there is no elevator to the upper level.

Usable areas

Sales	**yellow**	88 sqm	36 %
Service	**red**	44 sqm	19 %
Administration	**green**	13 sqm	5 %
Employee areas	**orange**	15 sqm	6 %
Supply	disposal	**brown**	82 sqm	34 %
Total		242 sqm	100 %

Other key information

Catchment radius	3 km
Distance to nearest pharmacy	3 km
Nearest health facility	Medical center
Number of items in stock	11,500
Stock turnover rate	10
Proportion produced in-house	2 %
Drugs produced in-house	Salves, uvula, eyedrops
Number of staff	5 Full time, 4 Part time
Prescriptions filled per day	120
Proportion of special services	1 %
Technical facilities	Air conditioner, solar protection

Nature of special services: lectures, facial analysis, manicures, cosmetics
promotions

The Vital Apotheke Strebersdorf is dominated by horizontal lines, which are particularly apparent in the wide counter and small dispensary. The eye is immediately drawn to the bamboo-veneered counter, behind which a gap in the wall-mounted shelves reveals the rear of the pharmacy with its red behind-the-counter display area. The shelves are positioned along the wall, with lighting being used to make items stand out strongly against the dark rear walls. Mobile gondolas, much lower than the other shelves, create a more informal feel in what is otherwise a rather hard-edged pharmacy.

Despite their contrasts, the surface materials are carefully matched to one another. The petrol-coloured shelf-backs have a calming effect and contrast with the slightly jarring red of the rear wall. The bamboo-veneered counter and storage module creates a feeling of relaxed warmth reinforced by the businesslike satinised glass shelves. There are no product labels or advertising displays to disrupt the simplicity of the redesigned interior.

THILO WOLF

VITAL APOTHEKE STREBERSDORF
VIENNA | A

REDESIGN

URBAN PHARMACY

MEDIUM-SIZED
PHARMACY

URB

MED

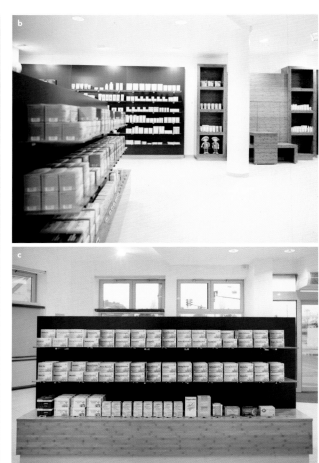

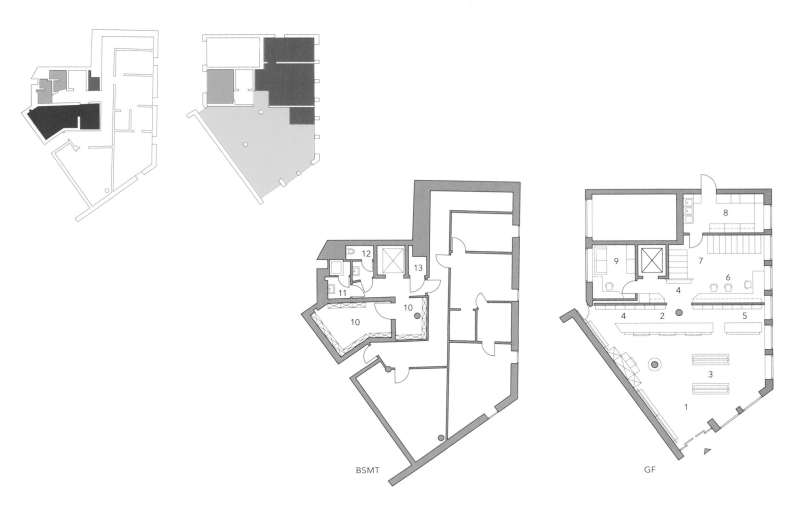

BSMT

GF

Client | operator	Neumann & Leskova KG
Design phase	10 2004 – 02 2005
Built	03 2005 – 09 2005
Usable surface	189 sqm

a A gap in the shelves behind the till gives a view of a red wall of non-self-service products.
b The dark shelf-backs and subtle lighting make the products stand out sharply.
c Mobile gondolas create a more informal feel in what is otherwise a rather hard-edged pharmacy.
d The interior is dominated by horizontals, the most obvious being those of the wide counter.

Diagrammatic plans, to scale 1:400
Floor plans, to scale 1:200

Floor layout

1	Sales area	**5**	Prescription area	**10**	Product storage
2	Cash desk	**6**	Workstation	**11**	Shower
3	Self-service area	**7**	Alphabetic storage	**12**	Bathroom
4	Behind-the-counter shelves	**8**	Laboratory	**13**	Plant room
		9	Night shift room		

This small pharmacy is almost perfectly laid out and lit, with a central elevator connecting the first floor and the basement storages and bathrooms. The night service area is used as a staff lounge. There is no office, so paperwork has to be dealt with at the individual workstations.

Usable areas

Sales	**yellow**	90 sqm	48 %
Service	**red**	52 sqm	28 %
Employee areas	**orange**	21 sqm	11 %
Supply | disposal	**brown**	23 sqm	11 %
Plant	**blue**	3 sqm	2 %
Total		189 sqm	100 %

Other key information

Catchment radius	1 km
Distance to nearest pharmacy	610 m
Nearest health facility	Medical practice
Number of items in stock	5,500
Proportion produced in-house	3 %
Drugs produced in-house	Teas, uvula, eyedrops
Number of staff	4 Full time, 5 Part time
Proportion of special services	10 %
Technical facilities	Air conditioner, elevator

Nature of special services: travel medicine, alternative health advice

PROJECTS

RHEINSTEIN-APOTHEKE, BERLIN | G
Architects: a-base architects, Berlin | G
Location of the building object:
Rheinsteinstraße 4–10, 10318 Berlin | G
Graphic designer | artist:
UVZ urban visual design, Berlin | G
Photos:
seyerleinundseyerlein, Berlin/Munich | G
Office furniture: Ikea
Lighting:
LTS Licht & Leuchten GmbH Tettnang | G
Flooring: Nora | Freudenberg
Bausysteme KG, Weinheim | G

APOTHEKE "ZUM LÖWEN VON ASPERN", VIENNA | A
Architects: ARTEC Architekten
Bettina Götz, Richard Manahl, Vienna | A
Location of the building object:
Groß-Enzersdorferstraße 4, 1220 Vienna | A
Heating | airing: Ingenieurbüro
Christian Koppensteiner, Vienna | A
Statics: Ingenieurbüro Oskar Graf,
Vienna | A
Design outside:
Jakob Fina, Vienna | A
Photos: Margherita Spiluttini, Vienna | A
Medical technology | office furniture:
Manigatterer GmbH & Co. KG, Peuerbach | A
Lighting: Die Spanndecke, Vienna | A
Sanitary facilities:
MAB Anlagenbau Austria, Vienna | A
Flooring: Steinzeit, Steyr | A

APOTHEKE SÜD, ST. PÖLTEN | A
Architects: bpw architektur, Vienna | A
Location of the building object:
Landsbergerstraße 9, 3100 St. Pölten | A
Lighting:
ERCO Leuchten GmbH, Lüdenscheid | A
Graphic designer | artist: Studio Krebs,
Vienna | A
Photos: Matthias Fenzl, Vienna | A
Furniture: Josef Göbel Tischlerwerk-
stätten, Fladnitz a. d. T. | A
Lighting:
ERCO Leuchten GmbH, Lüdenscheid | A
Flooring: DURAfloor Industrieboden
GmbH, Marein | A

VITAL APOTHEKE, VIENNA | A
Architects: bpw architektur, Vienna | A
Location of the building object:
Gatterederstraße 9, 1230 Vienna | A
Heating | airing | sanitary installations:
Heinrich Kerschbaum, Stetten | A
Lighting:
ERCO Leuchten GmbH, Lüdenscheid | A
Graphic designer | artist: Simone Kager,
Vienna | A
Photos: Matthias Fenzl, Vienna | A
Lighting:
ERCO Leuchten GmbH, Lüdenscheid | A
Flooring: DURAfloor Industrieboden
GmbH, Marein | A
Furniture: Franz Xaver Denk GmbH,
Niederalteich | G

ADLER APOTHEKE, KAMEN | G
Architect: Jörn Bathke, Berlin | G
Location of the building object: Markt 6,
59174 Kamen | G
Statics: Silvia Sähring, Berlin | G
Photos: Jens Scheffler, Berlin | G
Office furniture:
Ernst Rockhausen Söhne KG, Waldheim | G
Lighting:
Key-Light International BV, Nijkerk | NL

WILHELM APOTHEKE, BERLIN | G
Architect: Jörn Bathke, Berlin | G
Location of the building object:
Wilhelmstraße 93, 10117 Berlin | G
Statics: Silvia Sähring, Berlin | G
Graphic designer | artist: Berlintapete,
Berlin | G, Ulrike Haseloff, Berlin | G
Photos: Jens Scheffler, Berlin | G
Medical technology: Oer Inneneinrich-
tungen, Bakum | G
Office furniture: Schrage
Lichttechnisches Planungsbüro, Enger | G

DOCPLUS-APOTHEKE, BERLIN | G
Architects: b-k-i, brandherm + krumrey
innenarchitektur, Hamburg/Cologne | G
Location of the building object:
Müllerstraße 40, 13353 Berlin | G
Heating | airing | sanitary installations |
statics: Architekturbüro Feige + Partner,
Berlin | G
Lighting: b-k-i with Ansorg GmbH Lighting,
Mülheim/Ruhr | G
Photos: Joachim Gredhus, Bielefeld | G
Office furniture: Visplay International
GmbH, Weil/Rhine | G
Lighting: Ansorg GmbH, Mülheim/Ruhr | G
Flooring: Royal Mosa BV, Maastricht | NL

EINHORN APOTHEKE, HAMBURG | G
Architects: b-k-i, brandherm + krumrey
innenarchitektur, Hamburg/Cologne | G
Location of the building object:
Große Bergstraße 211, 22767 Hamburg | G
Photos: Joachim Gredhus, Bielefeld | G
Office furniture: Gütler Objekt-
einrichtungen GmbH, Heilsbronn | G
Lighting: Kreon GmbH, Cologne | G
LTS Licht & Leuchten GmbH, Tettnang | G
Flooring: DLW linoleum, Viva porcelain
stoneware [Sales area]

MALTESER APOTHEKE, DUISBURG | G
Architects: b-k-i, brandherm + krumrey
innenarchitektur, Hamburg/Cologne | G
Location of the building object:
Von-der-Mark-Straße 94, 47137 Duisburg | G
Statics: Ingenieurbüro Helmert &
Schumacher, Duisburg | G
Photos: Joachim Gredhus, Bielefeld | G
Medical technology: Rowa Auto-
matisierungssysteme, Kelberg | G
Furniture: Walter Knoll AG & Co. KG,
Herrenberg | G
Interior fittings: Hartenstein
Objekteinrichtungen GmbH,
Oberhausen | G
Lighting: der Kluth: GmbH, Hilden | G
SOMMER Licht & Werbesysteme GmbH,
Hilter | G, BELUX AG, Birsfelden | CH
Marset, Barcelona | ES
Flooring: Bolon AB, Ulricehamn | SE

ALPIN APOTHEKE AM KLINIKUM, KEMPTEN | G
Architects: Bürger Innenarchitektur
Klaus R. Bürger, Krefeld | G
Location of the building object:
Pettenkoferstraße 1 a, 87439 Kempten | G
Construction management: Martin Koch,
Stuttgart | G
Photos: Uwe Spöring, Cologne | G
Medical technology: Rowa Auto-
matisierungssysteme GmbH, Kelberg | G
Office furniture: Kraiss GmbH,
Bad Urach | G
Lighting: Ansorg GmbH Lighting,
Mülheim/Ruhr | G

APOTHEKE AM KLEMENSPLATZ, DÜSSELDORF | G
Architects: Bürger Innenarchitektur
Klaus R. Bürger, Krefeld | G
Location of the building object:
Klemensplatz 11, 40489 Düsseldorf | G
Construction management:
Alois Hembach, Bergisch Gladbach | G
Photos: Uwe Spöring, Cologne | G
Office furniture:
Küper Interior GmbH, Bad-Hamm | G
Lighting: Ansorg GmbH Lighting,
Mülheim/Ruhr | G
Sanitary facilities:
Villeroy & Boch AG, Mettlach | G
Flooring: Marmor Graefen e. K.,
Duisburg | G

BURG APOTHEKE, GREFRATH-OEDT | G
Architects: Bürger Innenarchitektur
Klaus R. Bürger, Krefeld | G
Location of the building object:
Hochstraße 48, 47929 Grefrath-Oedt | G
Construction management:
Alois Hembach, Bergisch Gladbach | G
Photos: Uwe Spöring, Cologne | G
Office furniture:
Flümann GmbH & Co. KG, Krefeld | G
Lighting: Ansorg GmbH Lighting,
Mülheim/Ruhr | G

OHM-APOTHEKE, ERLANGEN | G
Architects: Bürger Innenarchitektur
Klaus R. Bürger, Krefeld | G
Location of the building object:
Schlossplatz 1, 91054 Erlangen | G
Construction management: Martin Koch,
Stuttgart | G
Photos: Uwe Spöring, Cologne | G
Medical technology: MACH4 Automatisie-
rungstechnik GmbH, Bochum | G
Office furniture: Kraiss GmbH,
Bad Urach | G
Lighting: Ansorg GmbH Lighting,
Mülheim/Ruhr | G

APOTHEKE SCHNAITH, BURGDORF | G
Architect: Michael Claassen, Kassel | G
Location of the building object:
Marktstraße 41, 31303 Burgdorf | G
Lighting: Michael Claassen, Kassel | G
Photos: Aumeier Fotodesign, Fuldatal | G
Office furniture: Arne Peters, Burgdorf | G
Lighting:
ERCO Leuchten GmbH, Lüdenscheid | A
buschfeld design gmbh, Cologne | G
Zumtobel Licht GmbH, Lemgo | G
Flooring: Mittmann, Walsrode | G

PARK-APOTHEKE, POTSDAM | G
Architects: 3PO, Bopst Melan
Architects partnership BDA, Potsdam | G
Location of the building object:
Kastanienallee 27, 14471 Potsdam | G
Statics: STB, Potsdam | G
Lighting: DS Lichtkonzept Dietmar
Schlangen, Potsdam | G
Graphic designer | artist: Anja Laterne,
Potsdam | G
Photos: Philipp Meuser, Berlin | G
Furniture: Möbeltischlerei Heppner,
Berlin | G

APOTHEKE IM WESTEN, BIELEFELD | G
Architect: Renate Hawig, Dorsten
Location of the building object:
Stapenhorststraße 34, 33615 Bielefeld | G
Heating | airing | sanitary installations:
Reitemeier GmbH, Vlotho | G
Medical technology: Schulz Lufttechnik
GmbH, Sprockhövel | G
Statics: Borchard + Dietrich OHG,
Bielefeld | G
Lighting: Oktalite GmbH, Cologne | G
Photos: Moritz Brilo, Dorsten | G
Furniture: Wilhelm Wißmann GmbH,
Schermbeck | G
Flooring: Fliesen Brindöpke, Bielefeld | G

TRI-HAUS-APOTHEKE, ARNSBERG-NEHEIM | G
Architects: Renate Hawig, Dorsten | G
Dietmar Riecks [building conception]
Location of the building object: Möhne-
straße 9, 59755 Arnsberg-Neheim | G
Heating | airing | sanitary installations:
Vollmer GmbH & Co. KG, Arnsberg | G
Statics: Ingenieurbüro B. Walter, Aachen | G
Lighting: Oktalite Lighting GmbH
Photos: Moritz Brilo, Dorsten | G
Furniture: Wilhelm Wißmann GmbH,
Schermbeck | G
Flooring: Natursteinwerk Rinsche GmbH,
Anröchte | G

AUGE-GOTTES-APOTHEKE, VIENNA | A
Architects: KG ATELIER HEISS ZT GmbH
Christian Heiss & Michael Thomas
Collaboration: Dorian Gustavson,
Petra Hendrich, Isabel Küng
Location of the building object:
Nussdorfer Straße 79, 1090 Vienna | A
Statics: Herbert Endl, Vienna | A
Graphic designer: Christoph Nemetz,
Vienna | A
Photos: Peter Burgstaller, Vienna | A
Furniture: Wertheim GmbH, Uttendorf/
Pinzgau | A
Lighting: Klenk & Meder, St. Pölten | A
Sanitary facilities:
Markus Stolz GmbH + Co. KG, Vienna | A

APOTHEKE "ZU UNSERER LIEBEN FRAU BEI DEN SCHOTTEN", VIENNA | A
Architects: KG ATELIER HEISS ZT GmbH
Christian Heiss & Michael Thomas
Location of the building object: Freyung 7,
1010 Vienna | A
Statics: Herbert Endl, Vienna | A
Photos: Peter Burgstaller, Vienna | A
Gerhard Kassner, Berlin | G
Furniture: Wertheim GmbH, Vienna | A
Lighting: Nanu Licht nach Maß, Vienna | A
Sanitary facilities:
Markus Stolz GmbH + Co. KG, Vienna | A

ST. ANNA APOTHEKE [1828], MUNICH | G
Architects: Architekturbüro
Birgit Huber & Hannes Rössler, Munich | G
Location of the building object:
Falkenturmstraße 14, 80331 Munich | G
Statics: Ingenieurbüro Altmann + Littek,
Munich | G
Lighting: Christoph Matthias, Gauting | G
Graphic designer: ks_visuell, Munich | G
Photos: Markus Traub, Munich | G
Furniture: Franz Xaver Denk GmbH,
Niederaltaich | G
Lighting: Glashütte, Limburg | G
Ansorg GmbH Lighting, Mülheim/Ruhr | G
ERCO Leuchten GmbH, Lüdenscheid | A

LINDEN APOTHEKE, LUDWIGSBURG | G
Architects: ippolito fleitz group,
Stuttgart | G
Location of the building object:
Körnerstraße 19, 71634 Ludwigsburg | G
Graphic designer | artist: Monica Trenkler,
Stuttgart | G [Composition of ceilings]
Photos: Zooey Brown, Stuttgart | G
Interior fittings: Baierl & Demmelhuber
Innenausbau GmbH, Töging | G
Lighting: Ansorg GmbH Lighting,
Mülheim/Ruhr | G

ADLER-APOTHEKE, BERLIN | G
Architects: KINZO, Berlin | G
Location of the building object:
Breite Straße 41, 13187 Berlin | G
Graphic designer | artist: Tanja Lemke,
Berlin | G
Photos: Oliver Schmidt, Berlin | G
Office furniture: KINZO, Berlin | G
Lighting:
idl GmbH Lighting, Limbach| G
Flooring: Berlin Ausbau GmbH, Berlin | G

EXPANSION OF PAULUS APOTHEKE, "RED LOUNGE", VIENNA | A
Architects: Thomas Maierhofer, Vienna | A
Michael Stepanek, Vienna | A
[Redesign of the pharmacy in 2001]
Location of the building object: Land-
straßer Hauptstraße 171, 1030 Vienna | A
Photos: Thomas Maierhofer, Vienna | A
Lighting:
Möbelbau Sulzer, Altlengbach | A

APOTHEKE STADTKLINIK, FRANKENTHAL | G
Architects: sander.hofrichter architekten,
Ludwigshafen | G
Klaus Gutschalk, Oliver Löwer, Ute Wiese
Location of the building object: Elsa-
Brändström-Straße 1, 67227 Frankenthal | G
Heating | airing | sanitary installations:
PAV, Merzig | G
Lighting: EPL GmbH, Wiesbaden | G
Photos: Johannes Vogt, Mannheim | G
Medical technology:
Siemens Kommissionierungsanlage
Office furniture: Vielhauer GmbH & Co. KG,
Dannstadt-Schauernheim | G

HUMANITAS 21, VIENNA | A
Architects: STADTGUT
Nikolaus Westhausser, Vienna | A
Location of the building object:
Jedleseerstraße 66–94, 1210 Vienna | A
Photos: Klaus Rösel, Vienna | A
Office furniture:
Tischlerei Ehrenreich, Unzmarkt | A
Lighting: Wienlicht, Vienna | A
Sanitary facilities: Albinger, Vienna | A
Flooring: Aschenbrenner, Himberg | A

EINHORN-APOTHEKE, LINZ | A
Architects: Pia und Matthias Langmayr,
Linz | A
in cooperation with
[tp3] architekten ZT GmbH, Linz | A
Franz Moser, Grieskirchen | A
Location of the building object:
Wiener Straße 53, 4020 Linz | A
Photos: Dietmar Tollerian, Linz | A
Furniture:
Tischlerei Franz Moser, Grieskirchen | A

APOTHEKE "ZU MARIA TROST", KIRCHBERG AM WAGRAM | A
Architects: [tp3] architekten ZT GmbH,
Linz | A
Franz Moser, Grieskirchen | A
Location of the building object:
Marktplatz 15, 3470 Kirchberg am
Wagram | A
Engineers | photos:
Baumanagement Maier, Krems | A
Furniture:
Tischlerei Franz Moser, Grieskirchen | A
Lighting: Xenon Architectural Lighting,
Munich | G/Graz | A

ATRIUM APOTHEKE, SCHWANENSTADT | A
Architects: Florian Brand und Hannes
Huemer, Vienna | A
in cooperation with
[tp3] architekten ZT GmbH, Linz | A
Location of the building object: Salzburger
Straße 27 a, 4690 Schwanenstadt | A
Heating | airing:
Christian Brand, Ampflwang | A
Statics: Johann Obermayr, Holzbau,
Schwanenstadt | A
Photos: Dietmar Tollerian, Linz | A
Furniture:
Tischlerei Franz Moser, Grieskirchen | A
Lighting: Xenon Architectural Lighting ,
Munich | G/Graz | A

APOTHEKE "SOLARCITY", LINZ | A
Architects: Thilo Wolf, Johanniskirchen
Auer + Weber + Assoziierte GmbH,
Munich | G [building construction]
Location of the building object: Lunaplatz 1,
4030 Linz | A
Glass roof: Josef Schwaiger, Vienna | A
Heating | airing | sanitary installations |
medical technology | statics: GU Strabag
Lighting: Elektro Wallner, Linz | A
Photos: Klaus Mitterhauser, Micheldorf | A
Medical technology:
G&M Pharma GmbH, Braunau | A
Furniture: Klinger Apothekenbau GmbH &
Co. KG, Micheldorf | A
Lighting: Firstlight, Munich | G
Sanitary facilities:
Muggenhumer, Grieskirchen | A
Flooring:
Casa Sasso Steinmetz GmbH, Pucking | A

VITAL APOTHEKE STREBERSDORF, VIENNA | A
Architects: Thilo Wolf, Johanniskirchen | G
Location of the building object:
Pragerstraße 276, 1210 Vienna | A
Lighting: Fa. Göttingen
Photos: Philipp Horak, Vienna | A
Furniture: Klinger Apothekenbau GmbH &
Co. KG, Micheldorf | A

REGISTER
BUILDING WORK

REGISTER
CITIES

DÖRTE BECKER †

[née. Begemann], born in 1972, studied art history and conservation in Berlin. Freelance journalist specialising in 19th- to 21st-century architecture. Died in February 2009.

KLAUS BERGDOLT

Born in Stuttgart in 1947, professor of medicine, studied medicine in Tübingen, Vienna, and Heidelberg from 1968 to 1974. In 1980 and 1981, he went on to study history, art history, Byzantine studies, history of science, and the history of the concepts of health and medical ethics in Heidelberg and Florence. He has been the director of the history and ethics institute of Cologne university since 1995. His numerous books and other publications have been translated into several languages.

KLAUS R. BÜRGER

Born in 1948. He trained as a cabinetmaker from 1965 to 1968, and then studied at Werkkunstschule Krefeld from 1969 to 1972. He subsequently studied interior design between 1972 and 1978, and philosophy and German from 1981 to 1985, both in Düsseldorf. He established the interior design firm Bürger Innenarchitektur in 1981.

FRANZ LABRYGA

Born in 1929, professor of architecture, taught at TU Berlin 1974-1994. Many years director of the Institute of Hospital Construction, head of many committees, inclusive for Federal Health Agency and DIN. Member of Architects for Hospital Construction and Health (AKG). Numerous specialist publications.

PHILIPP MEUSER

Born in 1969, architect and journalist. Studied architecture in Berlin and Zurich. Author of books on international urban planning, architecture, and landscape gardening. Architecture firm in Berlin together with Natascha Meuser.

AUTHORS

SUBJECT INDEX

ARCHITECTS INDEX

The Deutsche Bibliothek lists this publication in the Deutsche National-bibliografie.Detailed bibliographical data available on the internet at http://dnb.ddb.de.

ISBN 978-3-938666-55-5

© 2009 by DOM publishers, Berlin
www.dom-publishers.com

Editing
Brigitta Hahn-Melcher

Translation
archiTEXT s. a., Luxembourg

Proof reading
Brigitta Hahn-Melcher
Mandy Kasek

Design and composition
Torsten Köchlin

Book-cover design
Nicole Wolf

Engineering drawings
Kristin Egermann
Jennifer Tobolla

Graphical drawings
Daniela Donadei

Photo credits
Arakon, Junus: 24f.; Aumeier Fotodesign: 131, 132/a, 134/b-d; Bau-management Maier: 199, 200/a-c; Braun, Zooey: 167, 168f./a, 170f./b, 172/c-e; Brilo, Moritz: 54/29-30, 141, 142/a-d, 145, 146/a-c; Burgstaller, Peter: 149, 150a-c; Burgstaller, Peter/Kassner, Gerhard: 153, 154/a, 155/b, 156/c-d; Cano, Richard: 60f.; Christie & Cole Studio Inc.: 16/12; DocMorris: 16/10, 37/6-8; Fenzl, Matthias: 73, 74/a-d, 77, 78/a-b; Grothus, Joachim: 89, 90/a- e, 95, 96f./a, 98/b-d, 101, 102f./a, 104/b, 106/c-e; Hofmeester: 216f.; Horak, Philipp: 213, 214/a-d; Klein, Stefan: 10f.; Locke, Sean: 16/13, 36/3- 4; London, Cat: 42/11; Maierhofer, Thomas: 179, 180/a-c; Matthews, Matt: 42/10; Meckel, Bettina: 22/6-7, 23/9-10; Meuser, Philipp: 7/1-3, 8/4- 7, 9/8- 10, 13/1-2, 137, 138/a-c; Mitterhauser, Klaus: 209, 210/a- d; Raths, Alex: 16/11, 42/9; Riehle, Thomas: 29/9; Rösel, Klaus: 189, 190/a, 192/b- d; Scheffler, Jens: 81, 82/a-b, 85, 86/a-c; Schmidt, Oliver: 175, 176/a- d; Schweitzer, Elena: 18f.; seyerleinundseyerlein: 63, 64/a-d; Spiluttini, Margherita: 67, 70/a-c; Spöring, Uwe: 21/1-3, 22/4-5, 23/8, 27/1-3, 28/4-7, 29/8, 109, 110f./a, 112/b-d, 115, 116f./a, 118/b-e, 121, 122/a-c, 125, 126/a, 128 b-c; Tobolla, Jennifer: 56/31-34, 57/35-37; Tollerian, Dietmar: 195, 196/a- c, 203, 204/a, 206/b-d; Traub, Markus: 159, 160f./a, 162/b, 163/c, 164/d-e; Twitty, Frances: 36/5; Vogt, Johannes: 183, 186/a-d; Weber, Andreas: 13/3; www.zurrose.de: 43/12-13; Yakovlev, Andrey: 30f.

Other images courtesy of the architects or authors.